USER PARTICIPATION IN
BUILDING DESIGN AND MANAGEMENT

USER PARTICIPATION IN BUILDING DESIGN AND MANAGEMENT

A generic approach to building evaluation

by
David Kernohan, BArch, MSc (Strathclyde)
John Gray, BArch (Melbourne)
John Daish, BArch, MArch (Berkeley)
with
Duncan Joiner, BArch, PhD (London)

Butterworth Architecture
An imprint of Butterworth-Heinemann Ltd
Linacre House, Jordan Hill, Oxford OX2 8DP

 PART OF REED INTERNATIONAL BOOKS

OXFORD   LONDON   BOSTON
MUNICH   NEW DELHI   SINGAPORE   SYDNEY
TOKYO   TORONTO   WELLINGTON

First published 1992

British Library Cataloguing in Publication Data
User participation in building design and management:
    a generic approach to building evaluation.
    I. Kernohan, David
    721

ISBN 0 7506 1296 7

Library of Congress Cataloguing in Publication Data
User participation in building design and management: a generic
    approach to building evaluation/by David Kernohan . . . [et al.].
    p.   cm.
    Includes bibliographical references and index.
    ISBN 0 7506 1296 7
    1. Buildings – Performance. 2. Architectural design – Evaluation.
    I. Kernohan, David
    TH453.U74   1992
    720'.23–dc20   91–44675
                                                                  CIP

Composition by Genesis Typesetting, Laser Quay, Rochester, Kent
Printed and bound in Great Britain

Contents

Foreword

Architecture may be the Mother of the Arts but architects are much more reliably the gateway of millions of clients and users to the mysteries and the occasional miseries of the Construction Industry. Ambiguously balanced between supply and demand, with one foot on the building site and the other in the client's office, architects are often attacked for what they cannot fully control.

Common sense would have made everyone but architects abandon this uncomfortable and arguably unmanageable frontier long ago: far better either to be clearly the builder's poodle or the client's toy. However, a stubborn ethic of independence has persisted to prevent such surrenders – an ethic which, I believe has a lot to do with the essence of professionalism, the willingness to take the long view and from time to time, for the common good, to say 'no' to both builder ('take that wall down') and client ('you just cannot do that').

Autonomy doesn't endear architects to princes or to contractors, both known to share a strong sense of the importance of getting their own way. Nor, it has to be admitted, have architects' ideals always stood up to the test of reality. In an increasingly complex and challenging world mistakes are easily made, perhaps more frequently than in the socially more stable and constructionally simpler past.

But who else but architects would admit their mistakes? Which other interested party in the increasingly litigious Construction Industry would go back to scenes of failure (and often of course relative success) to learn publicly how to do better? This is the significance of this most modest but most remarkable book. What it represents is evidence of the growing interest among architects worldwide in expanding, sharing and systematizing the body of hard won and practical knowledge which comes from studying buildings under the severest test of all – in use, through time.

Between the builders and the users, independent of each and yet comprehending both, determined to build better and to satisfy conflicting short and long term user requirements effectively but also with panache – this is the place for architects to be. User oriented and design based research is the knowledge base on top of which a better future will be built. *Ars longa, vita brevis*. This excellent book shows the way forward not only for architects but for all clients and everyone in the Construction Industry.

Francis Duffy

Preface

It is in the nature of democratic projects that they be projects of hope. They tend to assume the potential for human competence and in so doing make such assumptions self-fulfilling prophecies. It is also in the nature of such projects to both confirm and interrogate even the most mundane events, finding in them the opportunity to facilitate human competence, empowerment, and emancipation.

The generic approach to building design and management recorded in these pages is just such a celebration of the mundane, employing it in the emancipation of building occupants, owners and managers everywhere. Emancipation seems like a pretentious word when it is evoked in the development of a facilities maintenance program, or in the programming of a new facility for construction, or in thinking about how to use a place in a better way. It is appropriate, however, if we think of emancipation as a dynamic condition which requires maintenance through mundane acts of practice. The participatory building design and management approach developed in these pages show us a way to *practise* creating good relationship to place. Through such practice, occupant and manager relationships to place and to each other get better and better. They become more emancipated.

The approach to creating good relationships to the places proposed by the team of authors is not about the overt exercise of power by one group of place constituents over another. In fact, what I read and have experienced in working with this team is the type of enabling power needed for groups to accomplish things together. It is decidedly not about power over; it is about the power to do.

In an early review of the program used to test the approach outlined in this book, I recall asking some hard questions in workshop format with employees of the Ministry of Works and Development in New Zealand. How would the Ministry need to change its policies to accommodate the evaluation of buildings along the lines suggested by the generic methodology they helped to develop? The silence was heavy and frankly, difficult enough to be useful. The resulting discussion was both professionally rigorous in outlining the role of professionals in making and managing places, and interpersonally sensitive in acknowledging the problem of imposing professional beliefs and methods on lay publics. The resulting policies offered the best of both worlds. The policies that emerged kept the process of reflection on place simple enough for everyone affected by the program to participate in it. The policies also left room for specialized knowledge by creating a way to relate the implications of such knowledge to the everyday experience of building occupants and managers. In effect, the place and the experience of it became the basic unit of analysis rather than allowing a single discipline, profession, or management intention to dominate. The interpersonal relationships among the participants in the process helped to create conditions for the authentic practice of democracy.

The New Zealand experiment involved the evaluation of place as both an intensely idealistic endeavour and an immediately practical as well as efficient event. The methods provide ways to simultaneously collect and sort information about management, organization development, materials, space, equipment, interpersonal relationships, and more. The methods establish a generic framework, creating a forum wherein whatever appears to affect place can be revealed and critiqued. With lay participation in relation to professional insight comes commitment to the acts of caretaking that make ordinary places special as well as efficient.

The team of authors on this text has avoided several false choices common to our field of human environment relations. In writing for what they call 'users,' they do not advocate for the user over the professional but rather seek to engage such users in the process of managing their own environments with professionals. They do not choose between the short term and long term, between an academic search for new knowledge and practical strategies for making and managing places, and they do not choose between institutional and individual agendas. They tend to embrace the tensions inherent in such false dichotomies as a necessary and constructive part of their ongoing democratic project. In so doing they provide a way of working that gives multiple returns for each intervention and creates the possibility of new relationships between the professional, the academic, the lay building occupant/ manager, and the places for which they all care.

Robert G. Shibley
Buffalo, New York

Acknowledgements

We should like to thank all those people, especially building users, who have taken part in the processes and building evaluations described in this book. We hope they have truly benefited from the experiences.

The genesis of the book dates from 1979, with an initial research contract between the School of Architecture, Victoria University of Wellington (VUW) and the New Zealand Ministry of Works and Development (MWD) to undertake a study of methods to investigate user requirements of buildings. Those studies led to the development of the participatory building evaluation process described in this book. We thank all those colleagues past and present in both organizations who have contributed their advice and experience to the development of our ideas. In particular we wish to acknowledge the insight and experience of Bob Shibley, now of the State University at Buffalo, New York State, who has supported and nurtured our work from its earliest stages; and the support of the late Graydon Miskimmin, Government Architect, for his promotion of our work as it related to the Ministry of Works and Development.

The first draft of the book was prepared during David Kernohan's research and study leave as Visiting Scholar at the School of Architecture, University of Wisconsin–Milwaukee. We thank Gary Moore, who has contributed directly to our work in New Zealand, for his sponsorship of that appointment and for his support and assistance at that formative stage; and Harvey Rabinowitz for the use of his home as base while he in turn was on sabbatical leave.

We are grateful to many colleagues in the building evaluation field internationally. Advice and encouragement from our many contacts in organizations such as PAPER (People and Physical Environment Research) in Australasia, EDRA (Environmental Design Research Association) in the US, and IAPS (International Association for the Study of People and their Physical Surroundings) in Europe has been invaluable. John Gray enjoys a close working relationship with Gerald Davis and François Szigetti at the International Centre for Facilities in Ottawa. John Daish has collaborated with Wolfgang Preiser of the University of New Mexico on the preparation of bibliographical material on building evaluation. Peter Ellis and David Tooth, through Building Use Studies in London, have made direct contributions to the development of our ideas through their consultancy work on the reorganization of the MWD architectural consultancy, and James Powell, formerly of the Portsmouth Polytechnic School of Architecture, has also offered signal advice and encouragement. We acknowledge with gratitude the contributions of these individuals and our many other local and international colleagues.

Author profiles

David Kernohan, John Gray and John Daish are all architects who teach architecture at the School of Architecture, Victoria University of Wellington, New Zealand. Their research has centred on the development of the participatory evaluation process described in this book. They operate a joint venture design and evaluation consultancy service with Works and Development Services NZ Ltd, for which Duncan Joiner is Chief Architect (formerly called Government Architect). Duncan has played a full part in the development and application of the generic evaluation process, both as client and as a collaborative member of the research team.

David Kernohan, BArch, MSc (Strathclyde) worked with the ABACUS computer unit, Strathclyde University, Scotland, on computer-aided building appraisal. He also acted as consultant to the Building Performance Research Unit (BPRU). He then joined the Scottish Health Services Building Division, where he was responsible for a number of health building projects. Since 1977 he has been teaching architecture at the VUW School of Architecture. He was Chairman of Department for a 4-year period. He is a Council Member of the New Zealand Institute of Architects (NZIA) and represents the Institute on the Architects Education and Registration Board. He is the author of many papers and articles on building evaluation.

John Gray, BArch (Melbourne) has practised architecture in Melbourne and London, with special emphasis on office design and interior architecture. He teaches communication and management at the VUW School. He was a member of the design team that won the international ideas competition for the waterfront development of Wellington Harbour, and is now principal design consultant to the Lambton Harbour Development Board, which is implementing its outcomes. He acts as consultant to a number of design and management organizations, most notably the International Centre for Facilities in Ottawa, where he has been working on the serviceability of office facilities for Public Works Canada.

John Daish, BArch MArch (Berkeley) has a design practice background in housing and educational buildings. He was a founding member of staff of the VUW School, where he teaches architectural method and design. His interests lie with environmental behaviour issues and design education. He operates his own architectural practice, which he uses as a base for informing his teaching and research activities.

Duncan Joiner, BArch PhD (London) was Assistant Government Architect (Design) in the former NZ Ministry of Works and Development. He was responsible for the design of a number of major government buildings. His interest in building evaluation and participation in design stems from his doctoral work, which investigated spatial behaviour in offices, and from his experiences running New Zealand's largest architectural practice. As Chief Architect of the newly formed Works Corporation his concern is that the organization provides responsive, efficient and effective design and management services to its clients.

Introduction

'Ah! found you at last. It's a bit of a maze round here. Anyway, how do you like your new office?'

'Terrific.'

'It's certainly a big improvement on the last place.'

'Yes it's good. I love the smell of new carpet.'

'You've got a good view too with all that glass.'

'Yes, I could look out there all day. You can see the harbour if you stand just here. Mind you it's really cold first thing in the morning. Then by afternoon it's like a furnace – can't open the windows. The heating's all centrally controlled so I can't turn it up or down. It gets pretty stuffy too.'

'Oh! It's the same everywhere. You look a bit tight for space.'

'Yes, I had to get rid of my big oak desk. Too big. This room is smaller than my last one. With these two window walls it's difficult to know where to put all my stuff. Half of it's next door, while that office is empty. I'm not sure what they do in the open plan area. It was kind of foisted on us. The workstations are pretty small and by the time they've got their computers and manuals and all that wiring I'm sometimes surprised they can still find somewhere to sit. Still I guess there's not much we can do about it now.'

A conversation overheard: comments of building users. They are casual yet speak of underlying dissatisfaction with facilities. The speakers profess a belief in powerlessness. Nothing can be done to affect how the buildings that surround them are designed and managed.

Architects, developers, engineers, facility managers and others who provide buildings tend to think they have the answers about what people need in buildings. The providers say, 'You tell us what you think you want – we know about buildings, and we will give you what you need, trust us'. Unfortunately this is fiction. Current design and management practice is not well attuned to addressing the day to day issues important to building users. Building users rarely play any part in decision-making about their daily lives in the buildings they live and work in. Yet the people who really know about buildings *in use* are the people who use them – they are the experts in what buildings have to do. They are the true informants on questions of building use and serviceability. The trouble is, this information doesn't find its way back to the providers. The providers do have a great deal of technical knowledge that users don't have yet depend on; and users have a great wealth of experience and knowledge that the providers could use to do a better job. Sadly there is little contact between users and providers, too few opportunities for user knowledge and provider knowledge to be integrated. Users and providers apparently live in separate cultures. In this book we describe a means by which the two cultures can communicate, and together, through dialogue, solve building problems that persistently beset them.

The aims of our book are as follows:

- **What we are suggesting is a process for negotiating the quality of facilities**

We say that users and providers can and should negotiate the quality of the places they use. We have developed a generic process of participatory building evaluation as a way to bring providers and users into alliance. For us, negotiation has two components: discussion, and a means of reaching agreement. Often, but not always, trade-offs are made in order to reach agreement. The process is designed to be adapted to the specific needs of the people who use it, to be adapted for use in different situations. Whatever the circumstances, there are certain key principles and elements of the process that remain constant and consistent; but there are a few variables and options that require decisions in each case, make each case unique. The process is equally useful for any type and size of facility, for design proposals in preparation as for buildings in use. It can be applied to any built form or space that is used by, or intended for, people with distinctly different interests – users and providers.

- **This book is for building users, or more generally, all those who use built environments**

The book is for users of facilities so that they can articulate their needs and demands for quality accommodation, and gain power in dealings with people who supply buildings. It acknowledges the expertise of building users and offers them a means to be involved positively in affecting their surroundings. The book is an aid for users, user groups and tenant organizations discussing and negotiating on design and refurbishment options, leasing agreements and working conditions.

- **The book is also for those providing facilities**

Providers need new tools with which to respond to users' demands. People's expectations of buildings are increasing. They are demanding good working conditions and quality surroundings, more flexible and highly serviced buildings, and proper responses to issues of health and safety in buildings. Users are becoming more knowledgeable and, with that knowledge, more powerful. The salary component of a building's cost-in-use is substantial. An unhappy workforce working ineffectively or inefficiently is expensive. The process described in this book is a tool that may be used jointly by the providers and users of facilities. However, if the providers choose not to come to the party, the users may choose to use it themselves to address their demands.

- **So what is new and different about the process described in this book?**

The idea of evaluation is not new. Many professionals evaluate their work as a matter of course. Most evaluations conducted by professionals are either informal, based on inspection and professional knowledge, or systematic, based on checklists of criteria that are devised by the professional who conducts the evaluation. Our process is systematic but *non-directed and open-ended* as to content. Many detailed evaluations are conducted by 'experts' in a specific field of activity that is considered *a priori* to be the exclusive problem. Our process involves *multiple interests* in a facility and is *inclusive* because it covers any issue that is considered important by any of the interested parties. However, it does not exclude focused expert evaluations. The process has been tested in New Zealand since about the mid-1980s, and more recently in Canada. It is practical and cost-effective.

- **The book explains an inclusive approach to providing better building facilities**

Chapters 1 and 2 present our argument for developing a generic participatory process for building evaluation. Chapter 3 explains what happens in an evaluation. The process can be used in various ways in different contexts, for different purposes of building design and management. Chapter 4 describes some of these applications. Chapter 5 gives step by step guidance to anyone wishing to organize and facilitate an evaluation. Chapter 6 discusses the management of evaluations and programmes of evaluation. It begins by relating our experiences of 'institutionalizing' evaluation in a government organization. It then reviews building evaluation services and other programmes of evaluation, and comments on attempts to form corporate knowledge bases from the outcomes of evaluations. Chapter 7 discusses some of the lessons we have learned from our use of the generic evaluation process. We suggest that the key to integrating the knowledge of users and providers, to the benefit of all, is through shared experience, such as that promoted by the generic evaluation process.

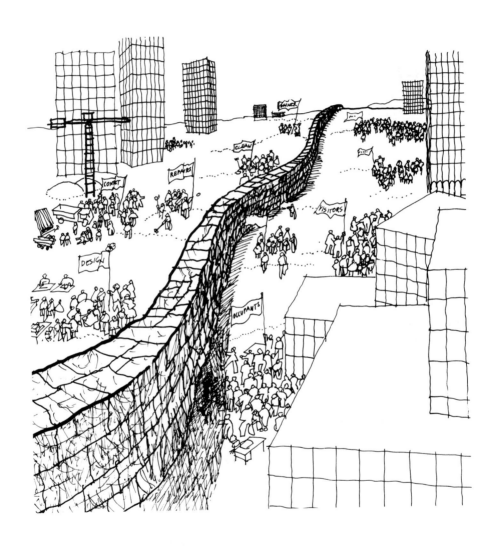

1

Users and providers: two cultures

All of us use buildings. As you read this, you are very likely using a building; you may be in the library, or in your office, or at home in an apartment building. Maybe, if you are fortunate, you are on holiday, sitting under a sun umbrella on the terrace of a rented villa. The kids are playing on the beach below, far enough away that you have peace, close enough that their happy noise tells you that nobody has drowned yet. The villa is furnished in a fairly bizarre manner, and the kitchen closely resembles the cupboard under the stairs at home, but at least there is a plentiful supply of hot water, and the living areas are big and sunny. In addition, there is a great taverna just down the road. The holiday brochures were confusing, and exaggerated, but didn't you choose well! Or was there just a hint of luck? The travel agent had not actually been there herself, and although she had sent others there in previous years, she had not heard back from any of them about the place – she suggested that no news was good news. Well, it's turned out OK, this place is just what you and the family needs right now.

When people use a facility,[1] they constantly assess its suitability for activities they wish to carry out. Is this room large enough for our meeting tomorrow afternoon? Do we have appropriate furniture? Is the 'atmosphere' right? Every new act of use is a form of assessment, and every re-enactment a form of reassessment. This process happens at different levels of significance and detail, and may be conscious or subconscious. It can take milliseconds or weeks to decide, and have short-term or lasting effects. For example, here is a relatively minor situation in a domestic setting, and a conscious decision is required. You move into a house or apartment and set up the kitchen. You decide where everything will go. Convention and experience help you decide. The pans go under the sink because that's where pans normally go, and where you have always put them. The wok won't fit there! Where can the wok go? An assessment is made, taking maybe some minutes. What places are available for the wok? Which one is most suitable? Is now the time to give up stir-fry cooking and banish the wok to the garage? Or do you now decide to cook almost everything in the wok, and store it on the stove?

Compared with the detailed question of where to store an object of everyday use, a more significant and enduring assessment is made when you enter a house or apartment containing various spaces to support and provide for your home life, including of course the kitchen, in which the wok and many other artifacts are to be stored and used. Such decisions are tough because until you have actually moved in and experienced the place, it is partly guesswork as to how suitable it will be as a place for the multitude of large and small activities of life. Later, maybe months or years later, you know. Over time, you find out what works well, and what does not work so well.

The more we use a facility, and the more familiar we are with it, the more we know about it. Such knowledge is based on direct experience of physical settings, gained while pursuing day to day activities. We do not just mean knowledge of technical aspects of a facility, such as how many electrical circuits are in the building, or whether the fire alarm system is in good working order, though it may include these things. Nor do we mean knowledge just of basic functional matters, such as whether the doors stick or the carpet is worn, though it may include these matters as well. We mean deeper knowledge that people acquire through use of facilities, such as the way to get around a building or the image projected by a facility. We mean insights about relationships between activity and physical setting that experiential learning can provide with such assurance. We call this 'users' knowledge' to distinguish it from conventional professional sources of knowledge about facilities.

The value of user knowledge

Here is a story that underscores the value of users' knowledge. Some years ago we were facilitating the evaluation of a police station in a country town in New Zealand. This event was designed around the idea of separate evaluations by different groups of people. Obviously we had no problem gaining the participation of one user group – the constables who worked at the station. But we were at a complete loss about how to gain the participation of another user group – the criminal 'customers'. This problem was solved by one of the local cops, who simply phoned up several of the 'regulars', and in no uncertain terms told them that they were volunteering to help evaluate the station. Thus set up, we began the evaluation.

The particular feature at the centre of this story is a public counter. The architects had designed a new type of counter, in response to a Justice Department directive to improve the public image of the police by making them appear more accessible and friendly. The counter had two parts – one high section suitable for brief interviews and for filling out forms while standing, and a low section, about normal desk height, intended to provide for more informal seated interviews (Figure 1.1). When the constables talked about the counter, they told us that the high part was fine, but the low section worried them because they feared that the toughest of their 'customers' could jump over the counter and attack them. Later, we met the group of volunteer 'customers'. They had a lot of useful comments about the station – how the cells were to stay in overnight, what the food was like – and they also talked of the front counter. To our surprise, they said that the high part was fine – 'like the counter at our local pub', but that the low section worried them a lot, because they feared that the police might jump the counter and attack them!

The public counter example illustrates the value of consulting users in processes designed to improve the quality of facilities. That counter design was never re-used. It was redesigned to suit the needs of all its users. The value of user knowledge has been at the core of our research and practice work over the past 12 years in participatory evaluation processes, and the reason for this book. There are two benefits from engaging in events like that at the police station, one obvious, one not so obvious. The obvious

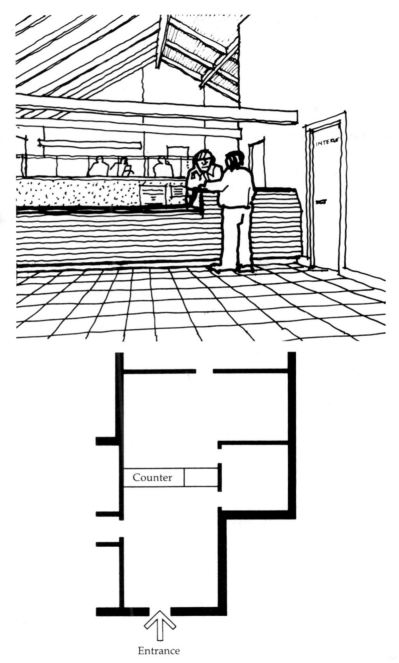

Figure 1.1 *The public counter at a police station in a rural community. The low section of counter to the left was intended to help improve the image of the police department, but it was disliked by the police officers and their 'customers' of the more aggressive type: each group feared the others could 'jump the counter'.*

advantage is that they generate information – there is feedback about what works physically and operationally, and what does not. From such new information, people are in a better position to decide on improvements to existing facilities, and articulate requirements for future similar facilities. Less obvious, but as important, is the opportunities that arise out of the dialogue between people with different, and maybe opposing, interests and values. With a facility as a focus, people willingly negotiate new positions that are mutually acceptable. Often, we have found, this is a healing process. The local police and the local gang members had confronted each other on many previous occasions, but when they came to talk about the very counter over which they felt they would clash, each group learned something of the perceptions and vulnerability of the other.

There is nothing new in these ideas. Much of what we are saying will appear self-evident. Obviously people come to know about buildings they use a great deal. Obviously it makes good sense to learn from experience and feed information back to the people who make buildings, so that they can do even better next time. Isn't it obvious that if people with different views of the world get together and talk, they will come to understand each other better? Surely these ideas are just some of the basics of good management. Yet, in our experience, they are rarely applied in the design, production, operation and management of facilities.

People who live and work in buildings are not normally involved in their design or construction, or management and maintenance. For most people who inhabit buildings, such jobs are done by someone else. Often these 'someone elses' are forgotten, or invisible. Think of the buildings that you regularly use. Think of the school, hospital, office, airport, shopping centre, apartment building. Do you know who designed these buildings? Who are the letting agents, owners, financiers? Who cleans the buildings, and when, and how often? Who set the standards for cleanliness? Who turns the heating systems on and maintains them? If something goes wrong with one of those familiar buildings, who would you contact to have it fixed? If one of the buildings is obviously in need of altering or upgrading to make it work better in relation to the activities that happen there, who does it? Excepting your own home, would you consider it your business to have anything to do with the design or operation of any of the buildings that are most familiar to you?

Most of us expect buildings to function reasonably well, and we tend to rely on professional and technical experts to ensure that they do. On the other hand, we are aware of problems with buildings that we regularly use; most individuals, if asked, can quite readily list problems they have experienced with the building in which they work. But, in general, people keep their problems to themselves, or are only vaguely aware of a connection between a difficulty with work and the setting in which the work occurs. Even when there is a blatantly building-related problem, many people will tend to adapt to the problem, or blame themselves for not coping well enough, rather than take the time-consuming and socially awkward task of 'bothering' the professionals or technicians.

One thing that is clear from our discussions with almost any group of users is a cynicism about the processes of delivering and managing facilities. Some users want and expect to be part of the action. They know they have much to contribute. Most are not sure that they have anything to contribute direct, because they are not sure that their experience is important, and they feel uncomfortable that they do not speak the same language as professionals and technicians who provide facilities. Some users are convinced that they should rely on the experts who are meant to know best. 'Aren't we paying these people to give us the right answers?' People with this mindset wait until a process is complete and then judge the outcome. Usually, they silently adapt to any problems; but scratch the surface, and you will often find real dissatisfaction.

From our practice experience we have learned that users of facilities think that 'someone' evaluates facilities as a matter of course, but they are vague about who does the work – some say architects, others think that assessments are likely to be done by local authorities, such as the city council. Few have witnessed an evaluation in progress, let alone taken part themselves. Most people we speak to about the idea of evaluation are astounded to learn that comprehensive evaluations of facilities are not done routinely by any professional group. Feedback is stated by most professional bodies as a service architects offer, but few, if any, do it as a matter of course. Many times we have seen astonishment turn to disenchantment and anger as the implications of this situation become clear to users. 'Don't they want to learn from what has happened here?'

It is not our purpose to attack any producers and managers of facilities. After all, we belong to that social and professional milieu ourselves, being architects. In fact, when we began our research into evaluation processes, we held the belief that architects could and should lead the way in collaborating with users and learning through feedback. Essentially, we developed tools of evaluation, then tried to sell the idea of participatory evaluation to assist designers provide better designs, and managers to manage and maintain facilities in better ways. We were wrong. The rewards structure is not appropriate, and the perceived risks are too powerful. At present, building designers and managers see no financial advantage in feedback, and fear that such activities will only expose them to negative criticism.

We are therefore convinced that we should be primarily addressing users of facilities *first*, and through them the professional groups, the providers of facilities. We believe we have a tool that is valuable in this regard, and that is well understood by both sides. That is why in this book we are primarily addressing users. The information provided will of course be of value to providers, as they learn from building users and wish to respond to their needs and recommendations.

Users and providers

We have been referring to 'users' and 'providers'. It is time to define and discuss these terms. Who are the users and providers of facilities?

The 'users' of facilities

The users of a facility are the individuals or groups with a presumed right to use that facility. Using a facility entails the ability to perform activities within and around it for specified or understood ends or objectives. The focus of users' attention is their own activity associated with the facility, and supported (or restricted) by the facility.

We recognize that all people are users of buildings. In differentiating between users and providers we are referring to the roles people take. In these roles we are sometimes user, sometimes provider. We have identified three kinds of user: occupants, visitors, and owners:

1. **Occupants** are people or groups who hold temporary or permanent rights of ownership or tenancy over a place. Tenants normally establish their right to use a place by paying rent to the owner, but in law (in English-speaking countries) a tenant is someone who holds real estate by any kind of right. For our purposes, it is appropriate to think of occupants as people who regularly and legitimately inhabit a facility, and use it for specified or understood purposes as individual occupants, both as owners and as tenants or employees of tenant organizations.

   The concepts of ownership and tenancy can vary significantly across different cultures. For example, New Zealand Maori hold a view of land ownership that is not easily understood by people with European origins. In essence, Maori see land as being beyond ownership. One can no more own the land, or any part of it, than 'own' one's mother. To the extent that land can be owned, it can only be so for a large body of people, a tribe – in the sense that a mother might be said to belong to her family. Analogous views are held by other cultures in many parts of the world. Occupancy and rights of occupancy are by no means universally understood concepts.

2. **Visitors** are temporary occupants. We distinguish visitors from occupants because they do not use the facility on a regular basis for extended periods. We think of visitors as people who 'make a call', often for part of a day, or are 'just passing through'. In some organizations, such as educational or business institutions, a 'visitor' may use a facility for weeks or months, but always, relative to the normal occupants, visitors spend little time in a facility they are visiting. Visitors' rights to use a facility are established by invitation, either explicit or understood. Visitors to public facilities such as museums or shopping centres presume a right of use, based on payment of an entry fee, a sign notifying free entry, or convention.

3. **Owner(s) and tenant organizations** are individuals or bodies with a financial interest in facilities. They may or may not be occupants of the facilities that they own or lease. They 'use' a facility in a sense that is different from the occupants who are undertaking activities in it. Nevertheless we include owners and tenant organizations as users because they purchase, select

or lease facilities in order to make money from them. An owner's role as landlord and a tenant organization's leasing of a number of buildings or parts of buildings for the organization (including naming rights) is separate and distinct – in that role an owner and a tenant organization become 'providers' of facilities.

In a general sense the concepts of 'user' and 'user needs' are simple, but there is an added dimension that is very important to notice if our goal is to create facilities of excellence – except in the case of totally private territory, such as a private house, facilities are used by more than one user group. Each user group has a set of interests in the facility that differentiates that group from the others. We have listed above the three main groups of user interest (occupant, visitor, owner/tenant organization), but also, *within and between* each interest group there may be different social and cultural layers that affect what a facility should provide and what behaviours it should support. For example, in a school there will be at least two distinct subgroups of occupant: the teachers and the students. In an office, subgroups of occupants might include clerical staff; middle managers; senior managers; professional and technical staff. Furthermore, within these subdivisions there may be social and cultural groupings that are distinctive. Countries, such as Britain, the USA, Canada, Australia and New Zealand, have in common the fact that they are predominantly English-speaking, but each of these countries also has a very diverse cultural and social mix in their populations, and therefore a very wide range of expectations and needs in relation to facilities.

The 'providers' of facilities

We coin the term 'providers' to categorize individuals or groups with a close connection to a building or other facility, but without a presumptive right of use to that facility. Providers deal in facilities: normally they are in business. Often their interest is transitory: they have an interest in the facility during one or other phase in its life – inception, construction, occupancy or disposal. On occasion a provider may return to the building to engage in further work – for example, a consultant space planner may return some years after the initial installation to replan an interior – but this continuing interest does not confer rights of use on the consultant, but merely reaffirms professional interest.

We differentiate four kinds of provider: makers, traders, landlords, and maintainers:

1. **Makers** include architects and other designers, suppliers, builders and construction crews. They are interested in satisfying their clients, the people who pay. They have a living to make. But architects in particular often express what they do as having strong moral justification. As well as being guardians of aesthetic quality, many profess a genuine concern for improving 'the fabric of society' and building 'better places for people'. They often claim they represent those without a voice in decision-making, and to 'speak' for society. An almost subliminal belief prevails that social behaviour is somehow directed through their work. Unfortunately 'speaking' for society, though attempted in good faith, is often based on serious misconceptions of society's value structures and of the relations between people and buildings.

2. **Traders** include the people who finance, buy and sell buildings – investors, developers, real estate agents, property advisers. Before any building project gets under way, analyses are carried out to ensure it is financially sound. The traders consider capital outlays, leasing potential, and financial returns on investment. The resulting brief may simply identify the type of building required to meet the investment return. There is usually very little about the practical needs of people. Buildings are built and traded for profit. Always the aim is to maximize returns where possible. Good building location and size are vital investment ingredients for the longer term, but maximizing occupancy can be important to cash flow. If users and user organizations are unhappy, or worse, cannot be attracted to a building, then there may be problems.

3. **Landlords and lessees** include owner, owner's agent, tenant organizations, facility managers. Owners and lessees make a commitment to building stock that may be significant financially and have a strong influence on their business operations. They require assurance that their capital and operational assets are being used efficiently and effectively. This concern may be only that the building meets all mandatory standards and is habitable. However, organizations with interests in a number of

buildings will wish to maximize use of plant and personnel across all their building assets, whether owned and/or leased. These concerns have extended the field of asset management to that of facilities management. According to the International Facilities Management Association (IFMA), facilities management is quite simply 'the management of one of an organization's vital assets – its facilities'. Facilities management makes it possible to bring the total picture of occupancy costs to the board level of landlord and lessee organizations. The Library of Congress defines facility management as 'the practice of co-ordinating the physical workplace with the people and work of the organization; it integrates the principles of business administration, architecture, and the behavioural and engineering sciences'.

4. **Maintainers** include building managers, cleaners, maintenance contractors and staff. Maintainers provide services usually direct to the owner or tenant organization. They may be occupants of the building they service or regular visitors. Thus, like owners and lessees, they are users as well as providers. However, their commitment to the facility is one of service rather than one of a wider financial investment. Because of their service commitment and 'dual role' as user and provider, and often their experience of other buildings, maintainers can tell much about what is good and not so good in a facility.

The two cultures of users and providers

We have concluded that users and providers form two cultures, based on demand (the users) and supply (the providers). These two cultures hold different values. They rarely make contact and often conflict, or would if it were not for the fact that one side tends to avoid expressing discontent while the other avoids acknowledging it.

Users and providers are alike in that they derive some advantage from their connection with a building, but different in the nature of that advantage. They have different values, goals and expectations, and different investments. The makers make their living from the trader, the owner from the client. The investors, developers, and their agents invest their money (or other people's) to make money. They will argue they have the most important interest in building. Without their investment there can be no building. Landlords gain advantage from the short- and long-term returns on their financial investment, while lessees make their gains from the use and profitability their organization can make from the buildings they rent. For users, choosing to work with a particular organization is a form of investment. Users have many expectations about the investment they make in their workplace. These expectations result from their reasons for doing the job, being in the building, and from their social experiences of buildings they have used. Users have personal and corporate images of their roles, positions in society, and work status. They are also concerned with the usefulness, convenience, safety and comfort of buildings for their purposes.

Both users and providers seek to have a building satisfy their needs, to gain some return on their investment in having an interest in the building. So any one building will normally have to meet a range of needs. The problem is that buildings do not normally satisfy the differing interests of various users and providers. Usually they satisfy one or another group preferentially. Very often the supply side dominates, because people on the supply side are accustomed to making decisions about what is built in their day to day work. Designers have traditionally served the owner–client. They build and move on. Managers have served the owner or tenant–client, managing their buildings as financial units. Designers and managers may both pay lip service to the needs of building users, but there is presently apparently too little immediately tangible return to designers and managers for them to make any substantial investment in the needs of users. In many places and many situations users are not being heard as customers with a specific set of needs that are different from those of the providers, and very often different from their needs as perceived by the providers. Equilibrium is based on power residing with the providers in terms of what is physically provided. Users defer to providers, partly because they do not understand the language used, partly because they expect the providers genuinely to address their user needs. Providers believe that they provide facilities that meet users' needs. Users know that frequently they do not, but feel powerless to do anything positive about the situation.

This is changing. Where multiple values operate, it is important that the values that count are addressed. There are now many powerful investment interests, and there is growing recognition that the investments of all those with interests in building must yield returns for all to profit. Occupants and visitors rightly demand good health, safety and comfort standards, as well as an environment that is appropriate to their status and expectations. Tenant organizations require such facilities. They want buildings that are capable of supporting the efficient and profitable operation of their organization. They want an environment that promotes the productivity and satisfaction of their employees. Tenant organizations, and through them building owners, are now more aware of the importance of users, if only as a significant part of their investments. Evidence is growing that providing well serviced, flexible buildings of better and more lasting quality is profitable for investors, owners and developers. Thus an unwillingness or an inability to address user needs is no longer disadvantageous to the user alone. It is disadvantageous to tenant organizations and building owners and, in turn, to designers and managers.

We have written this book primarily for users, because, despite indications of some changing attitudes among providers, we have come to the conclusion that only users can precipitate the real changes that are needed if there is to be a substantal shift toward articulating users' needs and delivering facilities that meet those needs. Without impetus from users, providers will not alter their ways of delivering buildings, or the values that are at the core of decisions about what is delivered. On the other hand, users cannot 'go it alone'. They need the skills and knowledge of the many groups of providers. In the next chapter we develop the argument for change and the conditions necessary to achieve an appropriate collaborative relationship between users and providers.

Definition

1 Facility, n. A physical setting used to serve a specific purpose. Discussion: a facility may be within a building, or a whole building, or a building with its site and surrounding environment; or it may be a construction that is not a building. The term encompasses both the physical object and its use. (Source: International Centre for Facilities, *Compilation of Terms Related to Buildings, Facilities and Real Property*, prepared for Accommodation Branch, Public Works Canada, October 1989.)

2

On moving the rock: the need for change

If users' knowledge is as available and useful as we imply, why is it rarely mined, as a matter of course, as part of the delivery and management of facilities? In this chapter we begin to explore the differences between the cultures of users and providers, question the assumed dominance of the providers' culture, and argue for dialogue as the key to change. Our theme is that the two cultures of users and providers are in conflict – a conflict of interests and values that, left unresolved, virtually ensures a mismatch between what is needed in facilities and what is provided. We say that the traditional rules and behaviours employed in the 'facilities game' have worked against both sides, but especially the users. We develop the idea that to resolve this dilemma requires participatory processes which bring users and providers together in negotiating the quality of facilities. The good news is that we have to offer (Chapters 3 to 6 inclusive) a practical, well-tested tool that supports, we believe, the provision of better facilities.

Different cultures

Users and providers form the two sides of a classic demand and supply equation. The basis of a healthy working demand/supply relationship is shared understanding of what is needed and what can be delivered. In this regard we see conflict between the users and providers of facilities.

By conflict we mean a clash of interests, a struggle between sometimes opposing aims and means, a conflict of ways of looking at the world. This does not mean that the two sides are at war, though at times it seems to us that they are on a collision course. We think that the most appropriate way to conceptualize the situation is to think of users and providers as belonging to two distinct cultures that happen to inhabit the same sphere.

What do we mean by 'culture'? For us, the following definition of culture by anthropologist Patricia Laing (1988) best describes what we mean:

> A culture can be simply and usefully defined as a system of shared understandings – understandings of what words and actions mean, of what things are really important and of how these values should be expressed. These understandings are acquired in the process of growing up in a culture and most become so thoroughly internalised that we cease to be aware of them, coming to think of them (if at all) as 'natural' or at least 'second nature' – not only the right but the only conceivable way of doing things, identifying 'our way' as 'the human way'.

Table 2.1 contrasts some of the principal differences between the two cultures of users and providers.

Mismatch and disenchantment

Bob Shibley and Lynda Schneekloth have observed (1988) that 'professional socialization is difficult to challenge because it is presented and accepted as reality'. Providers think that what they do is right, and users tend to accept what they are provided with because they are led to believe in the expertise of the providers. Users who discover problems with their use of facilities are apt to keep their frustrations to themselves rather than blame the providers of facilities. In turn, providers tend to suggest that users need to be 'educated' into ways of 'correctly using' facilities, so that the facilities can perform as anticipated when they were designed. One pervasive example of this way of thinking is the advocating by most professional designers of fixed windows and air conditioning in buildings with large populations, while most users prefer

Table 2.1 Cultural differences: comparison of Providers' and Users' attitudes and beliefs with respect to facilities.

Attribute	Providers	Users
Quality: what makes a good facility	Formal and technical qualities and properties of a facility as an artifact, e.g. how it 'looks', or how assured 'the idea'	Relation between a facility and activity, e.g. how it 'works' in relation to intended activity and perceived needs
Finance: who pays, and (as perceived) for what	Receive money (directly or indirectly from users) for technical or professional advice/services in provision and maintenance of facility	Pay money (directly or indirectly) for using facility
Market forces: roles, values	Supply-side role. Increasing competition with other suppliers, but still a tendency to wait for demand to make itself known	Demand-side role. Gradually increasing a critical outlook in a 'buyer's' market, but still tend to take what is offered
Activity in relation to facility	Work *on* facility: work/career exists because of facilities	Work or live *in or with* facility: facility exists because of work or other activity
Reality: view of the 'real world'	View of reality acquired and maintained through professional training, associations and traditions, resulting in specific and predictable way of thinking and acting	View of reality based on direct experiences in operating in facilities; little or no formal training or knowledge about facilities; see facilities as 'background' to daily operations
Language	Technical: often jargon; narrow, precise vocabulary	Non-technical, loose, diverse, idiosyncratic
Knowledge base	Received, formal, documented; combination of education and professional experience	Experiential, informal, not documented
Perceived value of own and others' knowledge	High value attached to own knowledge and experience: 'we know best'; low value attached to users' knowledge	Low value attached to own knowledge and experience; moderate or high anticipated value attached to providers' knowledge: 'they must know best'
Self-image	Confident of value and correctness of own views and knowledge; self-image of 'expert'	Uncertain of value or correctness of own views; defer to 'experts'
Power to decide what is provided, to what quality	Considerable, derived through direct action, assigned or assumed authority based on expertise	Minimal, almost no participation in design decisions during the delivery stages of a facility; power limited to 'take it or leave it' points of decision

openable windows and supplementary mechanical ventilation. Who is right? The design engineers almost always win this silent battle between users and providers, although, even in countries with extreme climates, users continue to ask for openable windows. In one such country, Sweden, it is now mandatory to provide openable windows in buildings. When users and providers come into conflict, legislation is evidently one way to resolve the issue. But most differences between users and providers are being 'won' by the providers. Many are small,

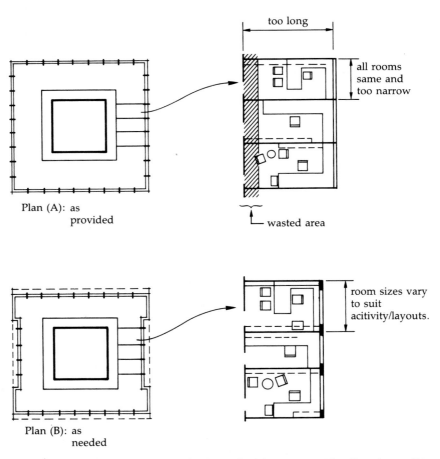

Figure 2.1 *Typical floor layout in a high-rise building to provide offices for staff in an educational institution. As provided (plan A), all staff rooms are the same size, too long and too narrow; as needed (plan B), rooms vary in size and are dimensioned to suit standard furniture layouts without wasting space.*

niggling, apparently minor matters that users feel embarrassed to mention. Some are big issues that will not go away. Conflicts, big and small, lead to mismatch between artifact and activity, and mismatch results in user disenchantment.

Here are a few examples that illustrate the potential for such mismatch and disenchantment.

Jacqueline Vischer and Clare Cooper Marcus (1982), in a study of award-winning medium-density housing developments, compared the values of the designers and jurors with the values of the building occupants. They asked each group to identify the criteria on which they judged the quality of the housing, and ranked the criteria in order of importance. The results: the designers and jurors agreed almost exactly as to the criteria they considered important and their rankings of them; the occupants also agreed among themselves what was important, and their rankings. Here is the twist: the two ranked lists were in almost total conflict. The

Figure 2.2 *Demolition: in some cases, the final solution to a total mismatch between user needs and the facility.*

most important aspect for occupants was maintainability. This was at the bottom of the designer/juror list. The most important aspect for designers/jurors was external appearance. This was at the bottom of the occupants' list.

Brent Scott (1987) in a comparison of aesthetic evaluation between architects and non-architects, exposed similar levels of agreement. Interestingly, his work suggested that as architecture students progress through their course of study, their preferences shift from a close alignment to those of non-architects at the beginning to those of architects by the end. Other examples of mismatch can be less direct, more subtle, the outcome of established ways of working rather than different perceptions of quality or value (Figure 2.1). On the other, hand user disenchantment with what is provided can manifest itself spectacularly or sensationally, and range from the demolition of unsatisfactory housing apartments (Figure 2.2) to the pronouncements of Prince Charles.

Whose values count?

In Chapter 1 we listed the main groups likely to have an interest in a specific facility. It is obvious that most facilities, apart from private dwellings and other single-purpose owner-occupied buildings, have to serve many interests simultaneously. An office building, for example, may have to serve its investors by providing a profit, its tenants by providing a tool for them to conduct their business, and visitors by giving appropriate controlled access to occupants. During its design and construction, and to a lesser extent during its occupancy, the same building is of interest to many provider groups and subgroups, including architects, engineers, contractors, suppliers, estate agents, cleaning and maintenance personnel.

These subgroups, whether on the users' or providers' side, have different values. For each of them there are certain features of a building, and ways of operating and managing a building, that will be important. Between different interest groups there will be a certain common ground, but also differences. A further complication is that people's values are not static – they change. You may be thinking that these statements are so obvious they are hardly worth making. However, the simple fact that values differ and change leads to quality mean different things to different people. This is possibly the biggest problem that faces the designers and managers of facilities. People with different interests in building have different forms of investment. They expect different returns. How they value the building depends on that rate of return. Designers and managers provide service. The returns on their investment in service are dependent on the value placed on their performance. For designers and managers it is becoming much less clear whose interests to serve.

Our first attempts

When we began our research into user requirements, we held beliefs that architects like us, and other design professionals, are best qualified to know what makes a good building. We started with the idea that the main purpose of building evaluation is to provide a check for ourselves and the client that the building meets the requirements of the original brief. We were not very concerned if the brief for a particular building was inadequate, because we thought we could plug the gaps by getting the original designers to tell us the requirements in as much detail as we wished. Traditionally briefs for building designs, whether for new work, for renovation or alteration, are prepared by the client and developed by the designers. The user has little or no input.

Much of our early work was devoted to finding reliable and efficient methods that would allow selective comparison between the requirements and the product designed to meet the requirements. The question was to what extent does a particular building perform in terms of norms and standards stated by the brief. Initially it escaped us that we were remaining in the provider's culture, barely relating our work to the requirements of users. In addition, we had in mind that if we were to conduct a series of evaluations, particularly of the same building type, this would provide a basis for an increase in our professional knowledge about facilities. For example, we supposed that we could gradually compile a body of 'solutions that work well', and a companion body of lessons learned about elements and features of buildings that do not work so well. The idea was to provide feedback, but again for providers.

A fallacy in this approach was the premise upon which it was based, namely that the architects, engineers and other provider professionals know best. As we became aware that the values of users and providers differ, we also realized how much user knowledge was a rich source of information about buildings. In doing so we confirmed that the values of people who use buildings differ and change over time, and began to understand that each building and its users was unique, especially as it related to its context, physical, social and organizational. We realized that here was a dynamic situation to which we were attempting to apply a static model. The fact that the value system of providers is substantially different from the value system of users raises the central question – whose values count? We are indebted to Bob Shibley for first opening our eyes to this simple but powerful issue. If there was a single point at which we began our exploration of causes of, and solutions to, conflict between providers and users, it was at the moment we realized the importance of this question.

The facilities game

If you have spent time with people whose business is building, the chances are you will have heard them refer to their job as a game – 'I am in the real estate game', or 'we are in the construction game'. At present the game is played only by providers. The users watch.

Each subgroup on the providers' side has different positions in the game. These games are hard to play: first, there are years of training and practice, and you learn the rules; then, when you become a player, the games are competitive, they are tough – but they are fun to play. You join a club – you are part of a professional 'providers' league, in which the players and clubs play the game for money. The spectators pay to watch the games being played, and follow the league. Their teams play for them, in a sense. Spectators know the rules fairly well, and will scream and yell a bit when they notice foul play, but essentially they have no direct control over the conduct of the game. When things go right, they go on being fans, but when things go wrong, consistently, over a few seasons – well, they lose confidence in their team, become disheartened, press for changes in the players and coaches, change teams, or become seriously disenchanted and give up interest in the game. Many users of facilities are very experienced spectators and knowledgeable about the game. Some want to take a more active part in directing how their provider team plays. Many have good knowledge based on close observation of many games, from a perspective, a standpoint, that only spectators can provide.

The really big question is how can the two groups, the two cultures, come into dialogue and mutually benefit from each other's unique knowledge? How can the providers, as skilled players, change their mindset to allow them to listen to the 'non-expert, non-playing' users? How can either group make the time needed to share their knowledge? By what process can people from each culture come to be cross-culturally aware and biculturally competent?

Towards cross-cultural awareness and bicultural competence

Anna Holmes (1989) has articulated five levels of awareness which she terms 'stages', and a set of intervening transitions in personal and group development of biculturalism:

Stage 1	UNAWARENESS	Little factual knowledge about own group; unaware of presence of other cultural group.
	Transition 1	Someone opens our eyes to what is happening. This is usually sparked by an event of strong import – an impact.
Stage 2	BEGINNING	Cultural group or individual is at a state of awareness that its culture dominates (or is subordinate). Among dominant culture, may be accompanied by denial of responsibility for the actions of people from the same culture who have gone before (the parents and grandparents). People in weaker culture become aware that they are less powerful, but have potential for power.

Transition 2		Know self: primary identity with own group or self.
Stage 3	CONSCIOUS	Consciously and constantly aware of cultural differences; decision to learn about others' culture. May result in a sense of excitement, plus denial, rejection, sadness, feeling of powerlessness, anger, or pain.
Transition 3		Learn to value cultural diversity; recognize that all cultures have some ways of doing things that need to be changed, some which are worth valuing.
Stage 4	CONSOLIDATED	Committed to working towards a better understanding among various groups, and methods for achieving this are actively sought. Know other language. People who reach this stage may find themselves in a quandary – should they work to strengthen their own culture, or the other(s)?
Transition 4		Primary identification with humankind, rather than own culture.
Stage 5	TRANSCENDENT	Awareness and sensitivity that have grown out of ability to seek and reflect on lessons from cross-cultural experience.

Some of the skills needed for growth of the type outlined are lateral thinking, active listening, assertiveness and negotiation skills. In discussing paradigm conflict, Schneekloth and Shibley suggest three possibilities (1987):

1. Persuade one side to adopt the position of the other
2. Compromise both positions
3. Jointly make a third shared position

Controlled chaos: towards collaboration of users and providers

What is the likelihood of change along the lines we have outlined? Certainly building owners, designers and employers are beginning to realize that occupant satisfaction is important. The salary component of a building's cost-in-use is undoubtedly an incentive in commercial situations, where substantial and inefficient or ineffective use of staff is a crippling expense. A common rule of thumb used to compare major costs over the lifetime of a building is the 1:10:100 rule – that operating costs (energy, maintenance, rates) are approximately 10 per cent of the total cost of a building (capital and rentals), which is in turn approximately 10 per cent of the salaries paid to employees over the life of the building. It can be argued therefore that an improvement in productivity of 0.1 per cent over the life of a building will more than pay for its initial cost. The emergence of facilities managers as a professional group also signals recognition of the need to manage building assets well. However, like designers, they lack tools to address the human concerns of all users of buildings direct. We are addressing here the concept of quality in facilities. As Franklin Becker (1990) says, 'What an elusive concept'. Who are the people with legitimate interests in the quality of a facility and how can those interests be served? How can quality be measured, and in whose terms?

The job of starting a dialogue between users and providers may seem like trying to move a mountainous rock with a hand trowel. Because our intentions and expectations are continually being modified with changing social experience over time, we seldom, if ever, encounter spaces or facilities that are perfectly matched for us. The world is full of imperfect buildings occupied by imperfect social organizations. Our use of space calls for continuous negotiation between behaviour and physical elements, and negotiation between the intentions of the individual and social group. The idea that quality is negotiable has important implications for the relation between users and providers. 'To be effective, people involved in social change must also be involved in the process of generating knowledge about that change, in posing issues to be researched, in implementation, and in evaluation' (Lewin, 1946).

One means for bringing users and providers together is to develop processes that enable users, designers and managers, in fact all those with interests in buildings, to benefit from the social negotiation of building quality. Rather than working in isolation from clients and users as proposers of finite solutions synthesized from expert and scientific knowledge, it seems more sensible for designers and managers to become involved in a process of negotiation with clients and users to develop building solutions acceptable to all. We believe that in the participatory evaluation process outlined in the next chapters we have a tool, a simple lever that will help start moving the rock. In Chapter 3 we describe that tool and its use in practice.

3

The generic evaluation process

The process we have developed as a 'lever to move the rock' is based on the very simple idea of asking people what they know about a building. The process gives opportunities for different groups representing users and providers to focus on a building and determine action about physical and social issues in the building that concern them. Each group engages in a three-part process. They meet to agree the procedure for the evaluation. They then walk through the facility identifying and commenting on issues that are important to them. Finally, they meet to discuss and negotiate recommendations about those issues. We call the three parts:

- Introductory meeting.
- Touring interview.
- Review meeting.

These three events are the core of the generic process that recur at every evaluation (Figure 3.1).

While the core of the process is present in each evaluation event, each evaluation itself is unique. Each has its own pattern and is designed to respond to its own purpose, objectives and context. As we shall see in Chapter 4, there are a variety of purposes, objectives and contexts in which the core process may operate. The core of the process is surrounded by other events, which are directed specifically to the different building design and management purposes. So, we have a generic evaluation process that is used in various ways in different contexts, for different purposes throughout the lifetime of a building (Figure 3.2).

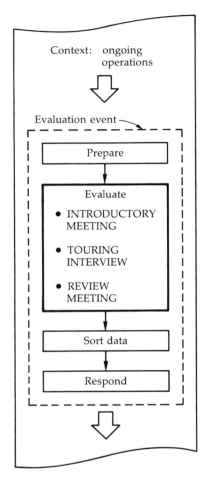

Figure 3.1 *Generic evaluation process.*

Who takes part in an evaluation?

Evaluation calls for three sets of people with distinct roles. Figure 3.3 illustrates who takes part:

1 *Participant groups,* who evaluate the building. They represent the different interests in a building.
2. *Facilitators,* who assist participants to make their evaluations.
3. *Managers,* who authorize the evaluation.

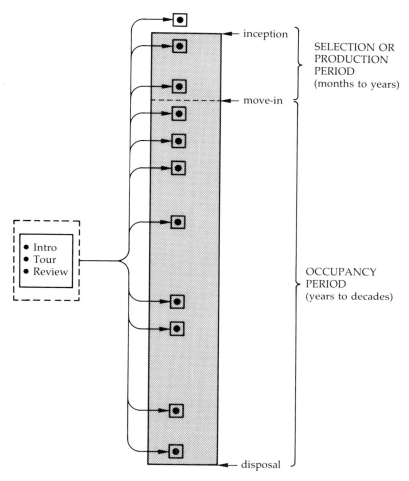

Figure 3.2 *Evaluation in use. The generic evaluation process can be used at many stages in the life of a facility, for different purposes.*

The participants are the building evaluators. Participant groups represent the different interests in a building, both users and providers. By interests we mean that a group has a common concern in the building. Thus, for instance, an occupant group evaluating a research facility may be drawn from the laboratory scientists in the building. The interests typically include those of occupants, visitors, owners, tenant organizations, makers, traders

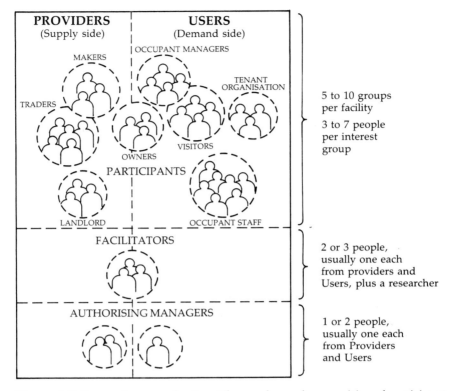

Figure 3.3 *Groups for an evaluation. The number and composition of participant groups varies with the context and purpose of the evaluation, and the size of the facility being evaluated.*

and maintainers. Each participant group evaluates the building from its point of view.

Facilitators do not evaluate the building or do any other kind of evaluation. They support the participants in their evaluation. Facilitators have a neutral role throughout. Usually there are two or three facilitators. Both participants and facilitators may play a part in initiating evaluations and monitoring outcomes, but their prime activity is the evaluation itself. It is only participants and facilitators who are concerned with the on-site activities of the generic evaluation process.

Managers are not normally concerned with the on-site activities, although they may be represented in a participant group. Their

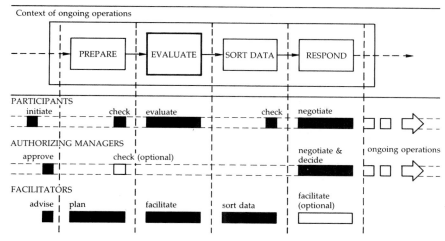

Figure 3.4 *Roles in an evaluation.*

role is administrative and supportive. They may initiate, approve and authorize an evaluation, and they have responsibility for ensuring there is action on the outcomes and for the ongoing management of that action. Figure 3.4 illustrates the respective roles of participants, facilitators and managers.

What happens in an evaluation?

Planning begins with the decision by someone to evaluate a building for some identified reason. There are many reasons for initiating an evaluation, some of which are illustrated in Chapter 4. Once the decision to conduct an evaluation is made, the next step is to decide who is to facilitate the evaluation. That normally depends on who has requested the evaluation, what its purposes are, and who is paying for it. Chapter 5 describes some of the attributes of good facilitators, and explains in detail the activities of facilitating an evaluation. Once selected, the facilitators must decide the most appropriate means for achieving the purposes of the evaluation, and prepare in detail for the evaluation event. Tasks include checking the mandate for the evaluation, proposing and inviting the participants and planning the evaluation programme.

The evaluation on-site, at the building, begins with the three core events of the generic process (Figure 3.5). The three events of introductory meeting, touring interview, and review meeting are repeated with each different participant group. Typically, there will be anything from five to ten groups, with three to seven participants in each:

1 *Introductory meeting.* To start the evaluation, the facilitators meet with the participant group to explain the evaluation process and the procedures of the touring interview and review. Participants are encouraged to discuss their connection with the facility and raise topics they wish to be part of the evaluation. The members of the group then agree on the route they will take on their touring interview of the building.
2 *Touring interview.* Now each participant group walks through the building with the facilitators. They visit spaces of significance to

Figure 3.5 *A staff group (users) engaged in an evaluation.*
(A) Introductory meeting

(B) Touring interview

(C) Review meeting

their interest and to topics raised at the introductory meeting. The touring interview is primarily a chance for the members of a group to discuss and reflect on their views of the facility. Standard open-ended questions are used as prompts, but leading or directed questions are avoided. Topics raised by participants are noted by one of the facilitators for recall at the review meeting.

3 *Review meeting.* This is where the essential negotiation event of the process takes place. Here, ways for dealing with the outcomes of the evaluation are formulated and agreed. Topics raised from the touring interview are discussed and formed by consensus into participant group recommendations for action.

Later, all participants may be brought together at a general review meeting to develop and agree on prioritized recommendations for action.

How can an evaluation be initiated?

In principle anyone can initiate an evaluation. You will need some help, possibly from colleagues, and you may need to check your authority to do one before getting started. The purpose of an evaluation and the amount of time available to put into it should also be decided early on, as this will help determine the specific way in which the generic process is to be applied. While an evaluation may be initiated by one person or group, the outcomes are dependent on the co-operation of all those who take part. It is not easy for any sectional or factional interests to exercise undue influence or take control. The potential for interpersonal conflict and concerns about bias are minimized by using the building as the focus for discussion, and through the essential neutrality of the facilitation procedures. In addition, outcomes are not predetermined by a single interested party. The process serves all interests, no matter who initiates an evaluation.

While a balanced representation of views and values is sought, this should not be seen as the same as seeking equity. Equity is not necessarily an outcome of a participatory evaluation event. Consensus is. In most cases managers, whether they initiate or authorize evaluations, retain the position of final arbiter of how and when an evaluation is conducted and how recommendations and action are to be responded to. Managers can usually be persuaded that it is in their interests to be supportive, as the process contributes to better communication between people in the organization, which is part of good management.

What are some of the benefits of evaluations?

In undertaking an evaluation it is important that there is a commitment to action as a result of the evaluation, and that resources and funds are earmarked for that purpose. Management, whether in the owner or tenant organization, usually plays a key role in assuring this commitment.

Evaluations are a rich source for data about people, organizations and building. Typically, evaluations provide multiple benefits by promoting action in two principal spheres:

- Physical.
- Social.

The physical and social benefits can be both short-term and long-term. Sometimes we have found it convenient to consider short-term benefits as referring to 'this building', that is, the building that has been evaluated. Long-term benefits then apply to 'other buildings', that is, other and possible future buildings of the type evaluated.

Short-term physical benefits usually manifest themselves as immediate physical improvements to buildings. Longer-term physical benefits can be applied to future building design and management decision making. Short-term social benefits promote better social communication and organizational management, while longer-term social benefits often come from attitudinal changes, which may support other collaborative ventures within an organization. We have found that most evaluations, whatever their purpose or emphasis, produce benefits that are physical and social, short- and long-term.

Two examples of evaluation illustrate these generic outcomes. The first tells two stories about the evaluation of a number of Junior Service barracks for the Army, Navy and Airforce. They highlight some short- and long-term physical benefits. It must be added that there were also considerable social benefits from the evaluations, not least an improved rapport between officers and men as a result of the collaboration. The second example is about the evaluation of an inner city office. It illustrates benefits gained from the social collaboration promoted by the evaluation process. Again, we emphasize that the story only illustrates some of the many benefits accruing from the evaluation. There were also many physical benefits, which addressed issues to do with the building's fabric, its maintenance and operation.

The Junior Service barracks were designed to a standard brief. Each building contained single rooms for thirty men, with a communal recreation space. The evaluations were carried out within a year of occupancy to fine tune the accommodation for its occupants and to help provide design guidance for a possible major building programme. The recommendations from the evaluations indicated that the new accommodation was generally very satisfactory and served its purpose well.

The first story tells how direct benefits were brought to the users as a result of their recommendation for a small physical improvement to their buildings. The TV area in the communal rooms of the barracks was a popular place at lunchtimes. The soap opera *Days of our Lives* played and the soldiers skipped lunch to watch each enthralling episode. Friends phoned around that time, knowing they would get a reply. The telephone was separated from the TV by only a thin partition that was not full height (Figure 3.6). The resulting problem was not so much that callers couldn't be heard because of the noise of the TV, but that the soldiers would turn down the TV to listen to the even more enthralling conversations with the caller. It was recommended that a sound baffle be installed above the partition between the telephone cubicle and the TV space. The work was carried out within days of completion of the evaluation, cost only a few hundred dollars, and preserved a number of budding romances.

The second story tells of long-term understandings gained on the re-use of standard building designs. One of the barracks had been built from plans and specifications prepared for a prototype building for a different user group, in a different location, in a different part of the country. Most participant groups in the evaluations made some reference to the peculiarities of the completed building. Some made direct comment on problems that

Figure 3.6 *'Days of our lives'. Life in the barracks can be just as enthralling as the TV soap opera: the telephone is just beyond the partition at the back of the TV – good listening when girlfriends call!*

the use of standard construction documentation had caused. For instance, sub-soil conditions differed significantly between the site of the barracks and that of the prototype. The barracks' foundations had to be totally redesigned, and yet some floor to ceiling heights described in the prototype could not be achieved in the completed building. The prototype was constructed with pre-cast concrete panels. While there was a contractor capable of providing an appropriate pre-casting service near the site of the prototype, there was considerable difficulty finding a similar service for just one new barrack building located in a different part of the country.

Other references were less direct. The 'heads' (toilets) were swabbed out with copious quantities of water. This was a standard naval practice, derived from shipboard life, but as the prototype had been designed for the army, there were no upturned sills at the toilet doors to prevent spillage. The toilets were swabbed out nevertheless, causing water stains on corridor carpets. This was a detailed problem again inbuilt because of the use of standard documentation. In total, the evaluation identified seventeen recommendations which collectively would persuade anyone that using plans intended for one function in one location on another function and location is fraught with real difficulties. A senior defence executive was heard to say,' If we'd known all this before, we would never have done it'. For the first time an evaluation exercise had clearly identified for the Ministry of Defence some of the problems of re-using building plans. The information was welcomed by policy-makers and their consultants in the Ministry, who stored it away for reference when such a building was planned again.

The office building in our second example (Figure 3.7) was occupied by a number of different tenant organizations, each organization occupying different floors. The story tells of short- and long-term benefits gained by the organizations agreeing to collaborate in the evaluation. Participants in the evaluation from one organization discovered that they were experiencing problems that were similar to those experienced by participants from the other organizations. They had never realized this nor been together to discuss it before. They decided that each organization had greater opportunity to influence the landlord to make improvements if they acted together, and not on an individual basis, as they had in the past. An outcome of the evaluation was

Figure 3.7 *A multi-tenanted facility.*

agreement that those people in each organization responsible for building liaison meet once a month to 'compare notes'. This had never happened before in an occupancy that for some tenants stretched over 20 years. In addition, one of the tenant organizations recognized that this situation repeated itself in many other buildings it occupied in other parts of the country. On learning what had occurred at the building evaluated, Head Office directed its branches throughout the country to negotiate with other occupying tenants for a similar collective arrangement. Head Office wanted to see tenancy groups in all the buildings they occupied collaborating to represent a common interest in negotiations with building landlords. Thus the same evaluation recommendation promoted both short-term and long-term benefits for the organization.

The examples illustrate that the simple idea of asking people what they know about buildings is practical, useful and rewarding. Generally we find that the recommendations of participants in evaluations provide knowledge that has impacts on buildings and users both physically and socially. The benefits are both immediate and long-term. The knowledge generated is of value to building users, tenants and tenant organizations. Such knowledge helps them with negotiations about working conditions and with decisions about the quality of accommodation they occupy or are considering occupying. Building owners and managers learn more about the best use of their resources to provide more cost-effective facilities. Design professionals are able to maintain their interest in a building from its conception to well into its occupancy, offering opportunities for continuing design improvement. The evaluation promotes dialogue between those who occupy and use facilities and those who design, own and operate buildings – users and providers. The benefits are many. They are specific to each interest group, yet all are derived from the same process.

In this chapter we have explained the essential characteristics of the generic evaluation process and the benefits to be derived from its use. In Chapter 4 we illustrate how the process can be used in various ways for different purposes to provide physical and social benefits in different building design and management contexts.

BRIEFING

FIXING

SELECTING

DEVELOPING
KNOWLEDGE

4

Applications: nine case studies

The generic evaluation process is flexible and robust. Each time it is used it provides many benefits: short- and long-term, social and physical. We use the process for many purposes in a variety of building design and management contexts (Figure 4.1). These purposes include:

- *Fixing* – evaluating occupied buildings for fine-tuning purposes, or troubleshooting in buildings with ongoing performance problems, including the use of specialist skills for focused studies of particular issues.
- *Selecting* – assisting the selection of accommodation from a range of existing facilities either for purchase or rental.
- *Programming* – as an aid to the briefing and design of new and refurbished facilities.
- *Developing knowledge* – as a means of gathering information to form a corporate knowledge database.

The generic evaluation process sets up dialogue between people with different interests in a building. Consistently we find that this dialogue effects attitude changes among the participants, reflecting growing awareness of the values of others and an interest in working collaboratively in the future. In some cases we have found such changes of attitude to be of more significance than the actual outcomes of the evaluations (physical and social) as they relate to their expressed purposes and context.

We have selected nine case studies to illustrate how the generic evaluation process can be used for many purposes, and how attitudes change as people become aware of other people's points

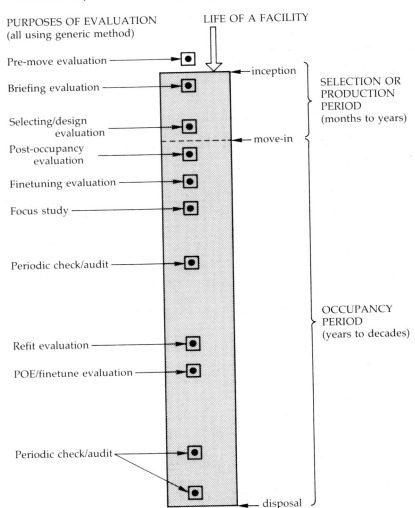

Figure 4.1 *Evaluation can be used for different purposes during the life of a facility.*

of view. Our first case study provides an example of a typical application of the generic process. It is one of many examples where the process has been used to evaluate a building in use. The other case studies in this chapter illustrate the scope for applications of the process. Later, in Chapter 6, we discuss more fully some of the issues of developing and maintaining knowledge databases. Gathering data for that purpose is an activity usually carried out by organizations with interests in a stock of buildings or with providing supporting services to such organizations and so we discuss it under the title of Evaluation and Facilities Management.

A typical application of the generic process

Case 1   Fixing (troubleshooting) a 1960s multi-storey office building

Our first case takes us to a seven-storey office building (Figure 4.2) occupied by eight different tenant organizations. At the time of the evaluation the building had been occupied for just over 25 years and had a long history of complaints about its functionality and condition. The first complaint was recorded just 3 months after the building's completion. The evaluation event was facilitated by two architects from the organization commissioned to 'fix' the building and one representative of the building owner. A member of our

Figure 4.2 *Case 1: a 1960s multi-storey office building in a low-rise Victorian and Edwardian city.*

research team was an observer. The evaluation event on-site took 4 days to complete and was followed 4 weeks later by a general review meeting.

The evaluation was conducted by ten participant groups, representing the various interests and organizations in the building. Eight of the groups were building users, representing the employed personnel of the tenant organizations. One group represented senior managers of the organizations, while the tenth comprised maintenance and management personnel of the owner/landlord. Preparation for the event had begun 3 weeks earlier, when the facilitators had met on-site to plan the evaluation event. They had been assisted then by the personnel manager of one of the major occupying organizations. She had described how each tenant organization operated and indicated the key people to contact for assistance when deciding who should be invited to participate. Most of one day was spent contacting people and checking their availability and interest. By its end the proposed participant list was complete, ready for formal invitations to be sent out.

We were 'warned off' one potential participant, because 'he thinks he knows it all and won't listen to what anyone else has to offer. Mind you, he will probably undermine what you are doing if you don't include him. Anyway, his bark is worse than his bite'. We decided to include him. At his participant group introduction he was cynical and troublesome. 'I'm not trailing round the building with you lot', and then, 'Well only if I can show you what I have to put up with where I sit'. We agreed, then we bribed him. When we visited his workplace, we discovered he had to use a broken chair. We arranged for it to be replaced on the spot. His attitude (to us and his co-participants) was transformed. By the end of the process, he was our greatest advocate (almost embarrassingly so).

We began early on the first morning of the evaluation event by meeting for an hour with managers from the major tenants. We confirmed our intentions for the 4 days we planned to be in the building. We then checked the room set aside for our introduction and review meetings and readied ourselves for our first participant group to arrive. The plan was to take each participant group separately through the generic process: introductory meeting, touring interview (Figure 4.3) and review meeting. On day one we managed three evaluations, one in the morning and two in the

Figure 4.3 *Case 1: a touring interview with managers from different tenant organizations occupying the facility.*

afternoon. On day two we completed a further two by lunchtime. We then had a break until the 'owner and landlord' group arrived. Some were from out of town and couldn't join us until mid-afternoon. We used the intervening period to collate the recommendations from the preceding groups and to take photographs related to the issues raised so far. On day three we completed three evaluations. We had found the early afternoon break the day before so useful for collating and sorting information that we asked the participant group scheduled for immediately after lunch if we could postpone to mid-afternoon. This was not a problem for them. The final evaluation, on the morning of day four, was with the participant group representing the mangers of the tenant organizations.

We conducted their evaluation in the normal manner of introduction, touring interview and review. However, when we had completed the review meeting as normal, we stopped for a tea break and talked informally with the managers about the events of the previous 3 days and some of the major issues identified. At this informal meeting it was noted by one of the managers that most of the issues raised were concerned with physical aspects of the building. He suggested if we could group recommendations into broad categories, it might be possible to tag responses to each with a cost estimate. He was aware that the landlord had in mind a sum of money that could be made available in the financial year for maintenance and minor capital works. Matching the two might be useful to participants at the general review planned for 4 weeks' time. There were over 100 recommendation statements. However, it did prove possible in the weeks before the general review to categorize them under broad headings such as environmental control, entry, workspace, staff facilities, maintenance. Recommendations agreed by different participant groups but with similar intent were then grouped together under each of the headings. The two architect facilitators from the organization commissioned to fix the building then prepared cost estimates for achieving the principal recommendations of each category. In the meantime the landlord stated what funds could be made available and when.

The general review meeting was attended by all participants in the evaluation. A number of other building users also came along.

Figure 4.4 *Case 1: the general review meeting – participants deciding on priorities among items to be fixed.*

At the general review the recommendations made by each participant group and their associated costs were displayed around the room on flipcharts for inspection and consideration before and throughout the meeting. The meeting began with a slide presentation to remind participants of the nature of each issue and recommendation. Participants discussed and ratified the recommendations and their groupings as presented. They then prioritized the groupings, given a summary of management attitude to the issue and time and budgetary constraints. Put simply, the meeting was told that recommendations under each of the general headings would cost about $40,000 each and that there was only in total $120,000–$130,000 available to undertake work (see Figure 4.4). The group of sixty people discussed the issues quite openly. They worked together to reword recommendation statements to reflect their priorities. The constraints and reality of the situation brought a pragmatic response to spending the money available in a manner that had the consensus agreement of the whole group.

Their recommendations included:

1 *Ventilation and heating.* It was agreed that a consultant engineer be appointed to make a more detailed analysis of the existing ventilation system. It had been suggested that by introducing some additional cooling units and more thermostats, many of the current problems of overheating and lack of control could be overcome. It was agreed the consultant should be briefed to investigate this specific suggestion as part of the assessment.

2 *Signposting.* It was agreed that there should be new and additional signs on the exterior indicating which entrance was the main one, that a new directory board was required in the lift lobby and at each of the secondary entrances, and that signs at each floor should correspond and be compatible with the main signs. Each tenant organization agreed that if the landlord took responsibility for getting the main public areas 'right', they would ensure that internal signs were consistent and compatible with those in the rest of the building. One of the architect facilitators offered to start work on the task the next day, if authorized. She was.

3 *Staff facilities.* The toilets on each floor were dark and dingy. The fluorescent tube lighting and predominantly brown paintwork were the major contributors. The landlord agreed that a repaint

was in order, and offered to make colour boards available within 10 days and to place them in the staff canteen so that occupants could indicate their preference. The landlord's maintenance engineer saw no problem with supplementing the lighting system with task lighting, and, when pressed, indicated that the fluorescent lights could be replaced with a warmer form of ambient lighting. He promised to provide indications of possible lighting options at the same time as the colour schemes would be made available.

Such recommendations are typical outcomes of building evaluations using the generic process. It is rare for anything impractical or unreasonable to be promoted. Senior management of course always retains the ultimate authority, but in over 10 years of applying the generic process we have never seen it applied autocratically. Consistently one of the most significant outcomes is that new understandings are created. People decide to work together more collaboratively in the future. For instance, it was at this building that the building liaison managers agreed to meet on a monthly basis. In addition, the landlord expressed a willingness to have a manager from his organization attend such meetings if requested to do so. One manager said, 'This evaluation process is such an obvious thing to do, why haven't we thought of it before?'

Applications at different stages of a building's life

Our next case studies are examples of the ways in which the generic process has been applied to different purposes through the lifetime of a building. Case study 2 shows how the evaluation process may be used not only in completed and occupied buildings but also with 'imagined' ones. Case study 3 demonstrates how the process can be applied to assist accommodation selection. After the selection procedure is explained, we describe how the accommodation is occupied and evaluated in use for both fine-tuning purposes and for conformity to the original brief from which it was selected. Case studies 4 and 5 also illustrate fine-tuning applications. They both show ways by which the generic process has been adjusted for use in smaller buildings. Two focused studies follow. They illustrate how specialist studies by environment behaviour researchers and building scientists can be implemented as a result of recommendations produced by the generic process. While they do not use the generic process itself explicitly, they do illustrate some of the process's principal characteristics of experiential learning and collaboration between facilitators and building occupants. Case study 8 addresses issues of refurbishment, while our final case study describes an evaluation programme whose purpose is primarily to produce guidance documentation.

Case 2   Programming – preparing a building design brief for a small research library

In developing this brief we were asked to consider the implications of advances in information technology on both the current and future operation of research libraries. We chose a two-pronged approach. First, we carried out evaluations of four relatively new existing libraries to elicit information about their characteristics and their successes and failures as perceived by their users (Figure 4.5). Second, but in parallel, we gathered technical information about the probable impact of information technology on research libraries by interviewing experts in the field.

The four research libraries were of similar size and function to the one proposed. Each library was evaluated by its users. We helped facilitate the evaluations with representatives from the client organization (a librarian and a scientist). The outcomes of these evaluations were reports recording space provision, layout and relationship information, as well as the recommendations of the library users at each facility. An emphasis on online data access, information reporting and the storage of short-term items only was noted. The recommendations from all four evaluations were summarized to assist the briefing of the new research library. In summary they were concerned with centrality of location; user friendliness, particularly as it relates to the pro-active nature of librarian activity and to the availability and use of information technology; open plan layout; and responsive services.

For the interviews of experts in the field we chose ten locally available people known for their expertise in information technology and library practice. Each was asked to predict the impact of information technology on future research library

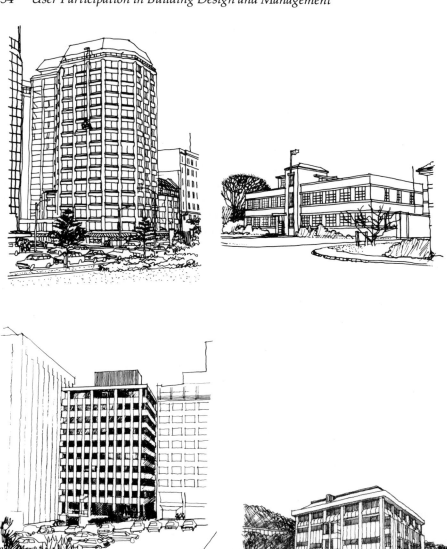

Figure 4.5 *Case 2: four facilities with research libraries, each evaluated to learn what works well, and what does not work well, from the users' perspective.*

practice and procedures, the roles of library staff and research scientists as principal library users, and the effects of these on space and resource provision. We got each expert to take part in three rounds of activity:

- Round 1 comprised an interview of each of the ten experts by a research assistant using a predetermined schedule of questions. The interviews were recorded on audio tape and transcribed, and resulted in a set of predictive statements.
- Round 2 consisted of a questionnaire in which the experts were asked to agree with and rank in significance the predictive statements established from all the first-round interviews.
- Round 3 had the panel of specialists discussing the predictive statements in the order of their ranking from Round 2. The aim of the discussion was to review issues and negotiate recommendations for the proposed research library. Predetermined categories of objectives, activities, space/environment and resources (Building Performance Research Unit, 1972) were used to classify the recommendations.

The process in this part of the study has some similarities to the DELPHI technique, a forecasting method that generates expert opinion on a given subject (Allen, 1978). It also follows the principles of the generic evaluation process in that there was an open data gathering activity followed by a review at which recommendations were negotiated.

The outcomes from the three rounds were condensed into a set of general recommendations to assist the briefing for the new library. The experts were concerned with the user friendliness of the technology; the provision of online access to a wide range of resources and of specialist information to the researchers at the point of need, and of support to library staff to help them actively market their services of information exchange.

The information base developed from the library evaluations and expert interview activities were combined to support an information exchange with the research scientists who would use the new library. Two workshops were held, attended by representatives of scientists, administrators and Head Office staff. At the first, the research scientists stated their requirements for information in their research activities. These were recorded. The recommendations of the evaluation and interview activities were then

Figure 4.6 *Case 2: workshop to describe activities and settings that would 'work well' in the new facility. The facilitators are developing the briefing diagrams (programming information) in front of and with the participants.*

presented. At the end of the workshop, all material, including the scientists' own stated requirements, was then made available to the scientists to give them time to familiarize themselves with its content and ideas, and to discuss its implications with colleagues. A period of 3 weeks was allowed for this assimilation process before the second workshop to negotiate the design brief was held.

The second workshop was in two parts. The first confirmed the need for a new building and discussed its objectives, whose design and operation for the new library were established by the participants, representing all interests involved with the project.

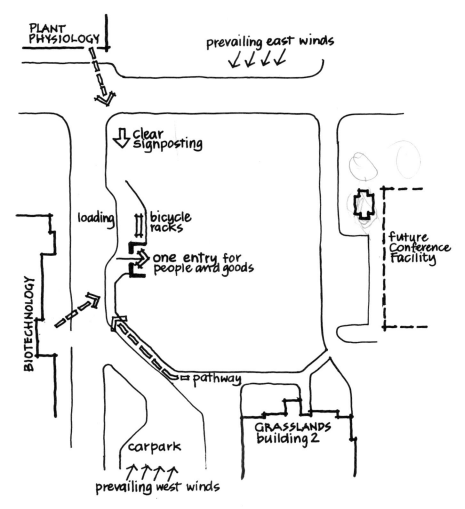

Figure 4.7a *Case 2: research library briefing diagram*

These were written on a whiteboard for all to see. The second part of the workshop was based round the idea of an evaluation of the imagined facilities. It built on the use of the behaviour settings of Le Compte (1974) and the diagrammatic and symbolic recording of descriptions of places of Sanoff (1979). Participants described the type and characteristics of settings that would support their

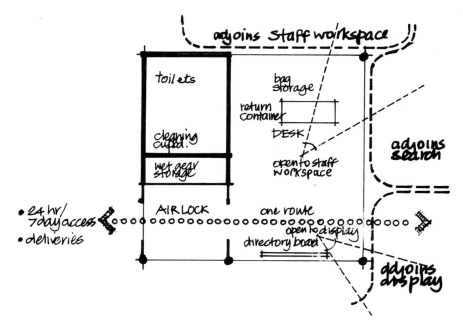

adjoins staff workspace

toilets

bag storage

return container

DESK

open to staff workspace

cleaning cupd.

wet gear storage

AIRLOCK

adjoins search

• 24 hr/ 7 day access
• deliveries

one route

open to display

directory board

adjoins display

Figure 4.7b *Case 2: research library briefing diagram*

activities and objectives. Descriptions of approaching the building, the building's image and relation to other buildings, and vehicle and pedestrian access, were sketched and diagrammed on flipcharts in front of participants (Figure 4.6). When there was general agreement about the characteristics of a particular setting, the group evaluated the qualities of that place and recorded their recommendations. Only then did they move, in their imagination, into the building further. The flipcharts and other written comments from the second workshop were later transcribed to form the design brief for the project (Figure 4.7a and b).

The outcome of the project is a design brief. The brief contains specific requirements as to space, content and equipment needs, and addresses behavioural issues concerned with the image, atmosphere and use of the building. It takes account of present needs and those of the foreseeable future in terms of the probable impacts of information technology on library practice and the needs of flexibility and growth and change. The brief is open-ended. It has been used for a student assignment, where over fifty design options for the research library were developed and evaluated. Some of these options were displayed at the library site and at the organization's Head Office. They have also been the subject of a third workshop, which has maintained the process of participation that will continue to the development of a firm building proposal.

Case 3 *Selecting office accommodation for a government department*

A major government department asked us to help with its search for new accommodation that would bring together, under one roof, a staff of about 300 people previously housed in six different locations. The department had placed the task in the 'too hard basket' for a time, because 'We really didn't know how to start to look for accommodation or what our needs would be. During that time we were being approached by real estate agents and developers offering us buildings. We had no way of assessing whether these were good or bad buildings and we really wondered how we were going to deal with this whole issue'.

We began by assessing the client's needs and then moved on to forming a brief against which possible accommodation could be assessed. We discussed with management what things produce a good fit between buildings and their occupants, including health and safety. Of course for us the greatest source for information about how an organization can operate in a new situation is the people who are affected by the change. We therefore directed our evaluation activities to obtaining accurate and comprehensive information on users' responses to their existing accommodation. We set about obtaining information from all levels of the client organization. Our prime activity was an evaluation of the major accommodation then occupied by the department. Ten participatory groups were organized to carry out the evaluation. They included groups of occupants, managers, cleaners, the designers and builders of the accommodation, the people who maintain the building and regular visitors to the department. The core evaluation processes of introduction, touring interview and review meeting were followed with each of the groups of participants and the recommendations negotiated at each review by each group were recorded and collated. They addressed how future accommodation should be, and covered not only the physical 'hardware' of the accommodation and how it worked but also 'software' items such as building operation and management, corporate policy and so on.

The outcomes of these activities formed an information base for the first brief, which was aimed at developers and agents with the intention of finding a suitable building. So topics were selected to deal specifically with building shell, structure and services, and less to do with fit-out and finishing. The brief described the ideal building from the client's perspective, emphasizing environmental quality as well as functional requirements. For instance, nine out of ten staff wanted to have opening windows, so that was prescribed. The brief was sent to about forty developers and agents, and proposals were received in respect of thirty buildings. A selection was made (Figure 4.8) from a short list, using an evaluation checklist developed from the first brief.

The fit-out of the building was designed by an independent architectural firm, and took the form of a full internal refurbishment. Interestingly the fit-out has won a number of architectural awards. Seven months after occupancy, the building was evaluated for fine tuning purposes. Again ten participant groups were identified to represent an interest in the building. Some had participated in the earlier evaluation of the Department's old accommodation. The facilitators of the evaluation event comprised two people from our own research team, the Department's facility manager and a Union representative. Our concern was with getting the building right for its users. The process of introduction, touring interview and review meeting was carried out with all participant groups. The whole evaluation was conducted over 4 days. The recommendations of each participant group were recorded verbatim and were later transcribed and categorized by the facilitators under keyword titles in preparation for the general review meeting, which was held 4 weeks later. Before that, we met senior managers to discuss the recommendations and their attitude to implementing them. Issues of policy, particularly with regard to

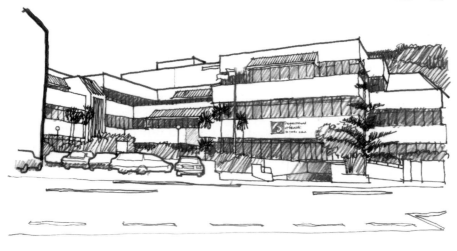

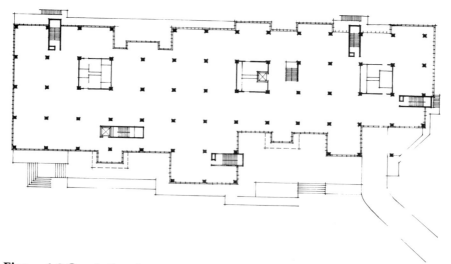

Figure 4.8 *Case 3: the selected building was one of four short-listed from among 30 options. Each of the short-listed facilities was evaluated in detail against the brief.*

space equity and workplace use, required consideration. Management was able to express its attitude to several possible scenarios to be developed at the general review meeting.

Over sixty of the 250 staff attended the general review (Figure 4.9). The meeting lasted 2 hours. Ten topics were identified for

Figure 4.9. *Case 3: general review meeting.*

discussion, and were shaped by the whole group into prioritized consensus recommendations for action. The principal recommendations concerned ventilation, space equity and workplace design. In this case the first brief had been explicit about the standards required of the ventilation system. The building's owners had previously accepted that the standards were not being met. Thus they were contractually obliged to achieve them. Participants at the meeting were informed about actions to date and the owner's intention to meet the Department's standards. Management acknowledged that there were anomalies apparent with space allocations for different sections of the organization. Owing to uncertainties about staffing levels and the re-use of an existing office furniture system, the open-plan work areas had been designed with a limited range of layouts, thus reducing the opportunities for customized spaces for individual staff. Some of the limitations of the generic plans of the workstations caused by the building services infrastructure and the furniture system were also explained. For many of the participants at the meeting these circumstances had not been known; they said that if they had been told earlier, they would have felt less stressed by some of the resulting inconveniences. Their mood moved from animosity to a certain degree of sympathy with management. All agreed that unit managers should now take pro-active responsibility for discussing and negotiating individual requirements for space and equipment as far as Department policy allowed. In a sense, lines of communication were re-established.

Other recommendations addressed issues of lighting, noise, signposting, meeting rooms, slipping at entrance, tea-bar layout, and safety. Finally a 'catch all' recommendation was made to ensure that all issues not addressed specifically at the general review would be addressed as part of normal building-management activity. The meeting concluded with some undertakings for work to be carried out being made 'on the spot'. Intentions for action in response to other recommendations were also declared and the mechanism for keeping staff informed of progress made clear. Senior management commented: 'The whole process came at a time when we were moving to a new organizational setup. So we found it really useful to look at the way in which we worked and the way in which we wanted to work in the future. The evaluation process made that possible'.

A by-product of conducting this evaluation was an interesting insight we gained into the benefits of participatory evaluation. We found evidence that major issues of concern to people might be overlooked if a general participatory approach was not adopted. In parallel with our participatory evaluation we carried out a direct comparison of the building's performance against the objectives set out in the first brief. We created a checklist of over 100 required items as stated in the first brief, and used this to check conformity in the occupied building. Only two or three failures to conform were identified. However, the impact of the items that failed, as identified in the participatory evaluations, was given much greater significance and importance by the participants. A failure rate of two or three items out of a checklist of 100 seems trivial at first glance. However, if use of the checklist had been the only approach to evaluating the building the strength of participants' concern with these issues would have been missed. The checklist showed us some of the limitations of evaluation methods that remain remote from users.

Case 4   Fixing (fine tuning) an inner city branch bank

Our next two cases illustrate ways in which the generic process has been used to allow completion of an evaluation event in 1 day. These approaches are usually only adequate for fine-tuning smaller

Figure 4.10 *Case 4: main entry to the branch bank. This was the first of about forty branches of the bank to be substantially upgraded.*

buildings and in organizations with a staff of less than fifty people. At an evaluation of a branch bank (Figure 4.10) the three-stage process of introduction, touring interview and review meeting was carried out with each participant group not sequentially as usual but in parallel. This was achieved with a form of 'self-help' touring interview, conducted entirely by each participant group itself, with the assistance of an evaluation prompt menu. The prompt menu listed questions the participants were to consider in each space. What happens here? What is important about this space? What works well? What would you have done again and why? If you could change things, what would you change, if only one thing? The introduction, conducted by the facilitators with all participant groups present, concentrated on explaining the use of the prompt menu.

The groups then set off on their own touring interviews, starting at different parts of the building to avoid crowding and confusion. The introduction and touring interview activities together lasted about 2 hours. The facilitators observed and supervised at a distance. Over lunch they worked to analyse the record sheets of each group. As issues were identified, they were written on a flipchart, with the relevant comments from the various participant groups noted beneath. An explanation of the content of the flipcharts began the review meeting in the afternoon, which was attended by all participants. The priority of the issues for discussion was agreed, and the meeting moved towards declaring recommendations for action in the normal manner of review meetings.

The branch was evaluated as an initial stage of planning a major upgrade programme for the bank's branches nationwide. The bank saw the branch as a prototype for its new image and layout, and was eager to know if its programme was heading in the right direction. The bank also felt that staff had a good idea of customer preferences and wanted to hear staff views. The major outcome was that the new image 'felt good' to the staff. A number of teething problems, primarily concerned with counter layouts, were identified, but there was significant pleasure expressed about the upgrade. The bank deemed the prototype a success, and immediately authorized preparations to be made for a number of similar upgrades in other locations. Suggestions for improving the counter design were noted. The evaluation process provided the information sought quickly and efficiently. It also improved management/staff relations; staff were impressed that their views had been sought and were taken seriously.

Case 5 Fixing (fine-tuning) a small rural meteorological station

Another form of process adjustment is again only suitable for use in small buildings with limited numbers of staff. In this case the approach has facilitators with some experience in building management or design walking through the building, discussing issues and responding systematically to a questionnaire or checklist about the specific, building type. They rely on their expertise to make judgements and recommendations. However, an essential part of their data-gathering activity as they move through the building is to engage as many building users as possible in informal discussions about their levels of satisfaction and dissatisfaction with the building. The facilitators then adjust their responses in the light of user comment. The facilitators' findings, tempered by their conversations with the building users, are presented to a review meeting attended by all those with interests in the building. The findings are the basis for discussion of issues in the building, though other issues may be raised by participants. As with all review meetings, the outcomes are the participants' recommendations for action. While this adaptation is essentially less participatory than normal, in that contact with various interests is on an informal basis only, the attendance, views and opinions of interested parties are essential to the review meeting. The views and opinions of the facilitators are only a basis for discussion and negotiation; it is still the participants who make the recommendations.

At an evaluation of a small meteorological station (Figure 4.11) the facilitators were set the task by Head Office management of finding out how well the building worked. Management firstly wanted to fine-tune the building, which had been in use for less than a year. In addition, it wanted to know what worked well and what not so well, as it was considering building two similar stations elsewhere. In this evaluation the main events of introduction, touring interview and review meeting took place over an afternoon and following morning. The introduction took place in the staffroom in the early afternoon of day 1. The facilitators and all the observatory staff introduced themselves, and the objectives and method of the evaluation were explained. All spaces were visited by the three facilitators during the touring interview, which took just over 3 hours. Activities were observed and users interviewed. Discussion focused on the items mentioned or pointed out by the occupants. User comments and facilitators' responses to the evaluation checklist were recorded.

For the review meeting the next morning the facilitators transferred the principal items recorded during the walkthrough onto separate flipcharts for display. The list was organized by specific rooms, with a 'general' category covering items about the station as a whole. All staff attended the review meeting. To begin with, they agreed the issues for discussion and their order, and over a 2½ hour period twelve recommendations for action were

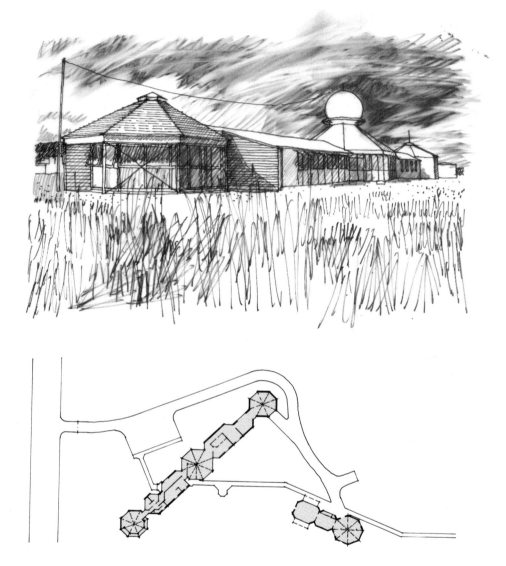

Figure 4.11 *Case 5: a meteorological station. This is a small but highly specialized facility.*

developed. Some of these were fine-tuning items. Assurances were given that they would be attended to. Others were advisory. The principal recommendation was that while the building's siting was reasonably satisfactory, it was felt that in any future designs issues of siting and orientation should be given more consideration.

In some ways the evaluation process as used in this case is similar to that of Steele's use of the touring interview:

'The touring interview is really a combination of observations and interviews. I ask a client to walk around his (sic) spaces with me and free-associate about what he sees and feels. I also ask specific questions from time to time, if he has not mentioned an element that I think is significant. However, I try to wait until the client has mentioned whatever is relevant to him, since I do not want my own set of significant elements fed back to me. The aim is to get inside the world of the user' (Steele, 1973, p. 100).

However, our process differs from Steele's approach in a significant way. While the interview is important as a data-gathering activity, it is in the review meeting which follows that major decisions about action are determined – by those with interests in the building, not by the interviewer.

The next two cases illustrate further evaluation activities as the result of exploratory use of the generic process. They illustrate the use of standard environment behaviour and building performance methods that focus on specific issues identified in earlier evaluations that used the generic evaluation process. Therefore the next two case studies do *not* illustrate the generic evaluation process in use itself.

The terms used for the different levels of evaluation vary widely. 'Diagnostic', 'indicative' and 'investigative' are used to describe a general level of evaluation, while terms such as 'specialized', 'specialist', 'directed', and again 'diagnostic' are used to describe evaluations of specific issues. We have selected the terms *exploratory* and *focused* respectively. Exploratory evaluations are open-ended, characterized by a lack of pre-judgement as to what are the important issues. Focused evaluations are characterized by the fact the investigators have specific goals in mind; they are designed to concentrate on the particular, necessarily to the exclusion of others. Though the techniques used in exploratory and focused evaluations tend to be different, the investigation of an individual building may call for evaluations at both levels. The exploratory process we have developed does not usurp or replace the work of specialists. Our process can be the starting point for the skilled expertise of specialists. However, there are dangers when specialists operate without a prior exploratory diagnosis of the patient. There is always a need to use evaluation methods appropriate to the task in hand.

Case 6   *Fixing (a focused study) – wayfinding in an office building*

The inability of people, particularly visitors, to find their way about buildings is a recurring problem in many public places. We consistently find issues of wayfinding featuring among the recommendations from our exploratory evaluations. Often the difficulties are due to a combination of poor layout planning and inadequate signposting. As a result of a recommendation from a previous exploratory evaluation, we were invited to investigate wayfinding in a government office building (Figure 4.12). We adopted a multi-instrument approach:

1 A wayfinding card ranking game (Figure 4.13).
2 Visitor tracking and interviews.
3 Staff interviews.

Participants for the first two parts of the study were selected from visitors using the building during the 2-day period of the on-site study. The data from the card game were analysed in pre-established categories by a different researcher, so that cross-checking of results from the two principal visitor instruments could confirm their validity and provide triangulation. The data from the tracking interviews were organized into categories of building features, social and/or physical, which helped or hindered orientation and wayfinding. The relative rank order results from the two principal visitor methods were then compared. Correlations and tests of significance between subject classifications and rank-order problems were analysed, using a set of statistical programs. The data from the staff interviews were analysed by qualitative content analysis.

While there are some limitations to this type of research design with regard to both internal and external validity, it was deemed sufficiently appropriate for its pragmatic purpose. We found that

Figure 4.12 *Case 6: an office building tenanted by government departments. In an earlier exploratory evaluation wayfinding was identified by most interest groups as a major problem of this facility. A second 'focus study' evaluation was conducted specifically to solve the wayfinding issue.*

Figure 4.13 *Case 6: operating the 'Wayfinding Card Ranking Game'. Randomly selected visitors to the building were shown twelve cards describing commonly experienced wayfinding problems. For visitors, the 'game' was to sort these cards into the order of difficulty experienced by them in this facility.*

orientation and wayfinding was a problem for approximately 25 per cent of all visitors, and that problems did not diminish on subsequent visits. Over one-third of all comments concerned this problem. Particular high ranking problems included:

- Lack of personal assistance in the main floor foyer.
- Too many doors.
- Destinations not visible.
- Stairs hard to find.

The data suggested that the single most important thing that could be done to alleviate orientation and wayfinding difficulties would be to locate a receptionist in the main foyer. Interestingly such a suggestion ran contrary to management policy. The study also suggested a number of other ways to ameliorate orientation and wayfinding problems in the building, particularly through specifically enhanced signposting, with or without the employment of a receptionist. The outcomes pointed out some of the linkages between the architecturally designed environment and the social organizational system of the building as they influenced orientation and wayfinding. However, management resisted appointing a receptionist and acceded only to modifying the system of signposting.

Case 7   *Fixing (a focused study) air quality in an inner city office*

Another study investigated problems identified previously in an exploratory evaluation concerning air quality in a city office building (Figure 4.14). The approach was in three parts:

1 *Assessment* – an expert multi-disciplinary group of facilitators, comprising an architect, a scientist and an engineer, visited the building to assess the tenancy and understand the building service provisions.
2 *Measurement* – equipment to measure the thermal environment was installed in the offices for a 10-day period.
3 *Analysis and report* – the expert group met after the site work to discuss their findings, reach conclusions and report verbally to building management.

It was recognized that the precise measurement of air quality and the establishment of minimal acceptable levels of pollutants, bugs, and toxins is still to some extent a matter for basic research.

Members of the multi-disciplinary group visited the offices during an afternoon in early spring to discuss the issue with building users. On the same day on-site measurements of fresh air volumes were taken (Figure 4.15). Thermohygrograph readings were also available at that time from records taken over the previous 2 weeks. At the end of the visit the facilitators met on-site to discuss and finalize conclusions. They subsequently met with the building management on the same day to communicate their findings. The conclusions and recommendations included:

- Relocate or rearrange the building's fresh-air entry or extract so that it operated independently under any wind condition (Figure 4.16).

Figure 4.14 *Case 7: An individual office in a building with 'air problems'. Over a period of some months the occupant of this office experimented with ways to improve the amount and distribution of air in her office. During the exploratory evaluation she demonstrated that she could detect more air movement if she taped up the return air slots next to the lights in the ceiling, and opened her office door just a little. A focused study was recommended.*

Figure 4.15 *Case 7: measuring the amount of ventilation air being delivered to a space.*

- Reorientate the building exhaust fan so that it did not have to oppose the prevailing wind.
- Balance the air circulation system across the floor to ensure an equitable supply of air to each room.
- Change the location of the temperature control from the return air to the supply air, and set at 12°C, as in the specification.

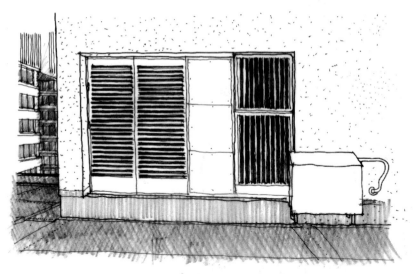

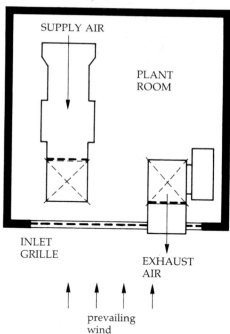

Figure 4.16 *Case 7: roof-top plant room for ventilation machinery. The outlet grille for exhaust air is next to the inlet grille for air that is supplied to the occupied spaces in the building. The result is that part of the exhaust air is mixed with the 'fresh' air. The problem is compounded by the prevailing winds, which push the exhaust air back towards the inlet grille.*

- Ensure each room had at least one perimeter heater connected to a single thermostat for that room and that this heater could operate with the air-handling plant in cooling mode.
- Review hours of operation regarding timeclock setting.
- Label the electrical distribution board.

These recommendations were well-received by management, as a confirmatory follow-up to the earlier exploratory evaluation. It now felt able to implement detailed responses to the recommendation from the exploratory evaluation to 'fix the air quality in the building'.

It is also useful to note that the mix of architects, scientists and engineers as facilitators in this case brought a variety of useful insights to the issue of air quality. It would be interesting to examine the outcomes of such an exercise where only one, any one, of these disciplines conducted the inspection alone. It was the view of the researchers in this case that a multi-disciplinary approach had been beneficial, had enriched the findings, had operated quickly and effectively and had produced recommendations in which they could all feel a measure of confidence. They had also found the building users most co-operative, as their work was clearly seen to be in response to an expressed user need.

Case 8   *Programming – refurbishment of a residential institution for boys*

Refurbishment is a regular occurrence in buildings. It usually means the redesign of existing premises, though it may also be part of a fit-out for an organization moving to new premises, as in Case 3. In this case study we illustrate again how evaluation can be combined with other participatory techniques to help negotiate a responsive design brief. The case concerns the establishment of requirements for change to a residential institutional school for boys (Figure 4.17). The approach combined use of the generic evaluation process with participatory planning models adapted from the work of Davis (1982), Sanoff (1978), and Schneekloth and Shibley (1981).

The evaluation and negotiation event occurred over 2 days, and six groups took part – three groups representing the boys, two representing the staff of the school, and one representing the Head

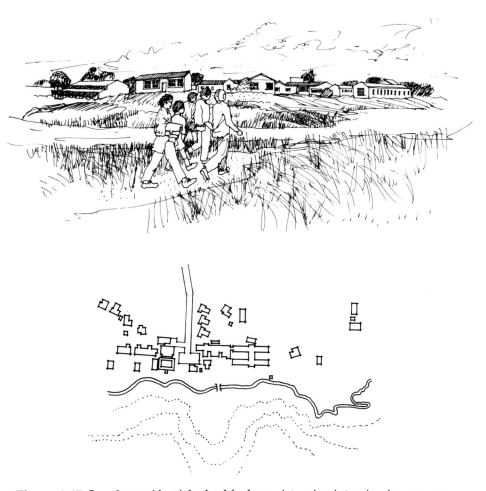

Figure 4.17 *Case 8: a residential school for boys. A touring interview in progress with a group of residents.*

Office social welfare organization. The procedures took account of the cultural differences of participants and their levels of knowledge and experience. Steps were taken to inform all those to be involved in the evaluation about what was to happen to help engender a positive approach from participants. These steps included a visit by one of the facilitators to the school to explain to the boys what was to happen and to encourage them to contribute their ideas. In this event there were three facilitators – two members of the research team and an architect member of the appointed design organization. Each evaluation followed the generic process. The touring interviews were conducted in two rounds in parallel, with only one facilitator accompanying each participant group. Participants were encouraged to talk about whatever they found important, while the facilitators prompted with open-ended questions. In the review meeting attended by all participants discussion led to the identification of issues and recommendations, which were listed in their final agreed wording on flipcharts.

The review meeting was then structured as two 'games'. The Ideas Game was used to answer 'What do we want to achieve, how can the school help us?' and to match recommendations with objectives. This was tackled individually at first, then in participant groups, and finally in a plenary session by all groups. A starter list with some twenty objectives based on the recommendations from the evaluation activity was used as a base from which participants could change, adapt or add alternatives. Each participant group negotiated its four most important objectives.

In the plenary session that followed, the different groups' objectives were compared and discussed. Next groups were asked to match no more than seven of their favourite evaluation recommendations with their four most important objectives. Groups identified relationships between their objectives and recommendations, using a matrix. Self-adhesive red dots were used to indicate the strength of the relationship. Again the facilitators conducted a plenary session, to identify patterns in relationships indicated by dots on the matrices. For example, on the matrix made by one of the residents' groups the objective of a cared-for place was strongly supported by five of the seven recommendations, whereas the objective to develop settings for contact with families and friends was not specifically enhanced by any of the recommendations.

The Planning Game (Figure 4.18) enabled each participant group to annotate a planning map with symbolic stickers, using:

- ○   to indicate change – we want to change this somehow;
- ♡   to indicate keep – we want to keep this/we love it;
- ★   to rate the priority an item has for action – immediately (★★★), soon (★★), or long-term (★)

Figure 4.18 *The Planning Game.*

In some cases groups assigned round red dots to heart items, which indicated that although they wanted them retained, they would also like to see enhanced by improvement or addition. For instance, comment was made about the sand dunes – 'We love them but would like some landscaping and some shelters'. Most aspects that were perceived as those needing change were physical or environmental as opposed to organizational or behavioural. Participants came together for a final session to compare annotated maps, note the degree of consensus achieved, note or resolve any further issues raised and discuss future action.

The games focused on priorities. In some cases features were directly assigned priorities by groups, e.g. in the planning game priority was indicated by the number of star stickers. In other cases priorities were negotiated by participants within the group or at plenary sessions. As a result seven priority recommendations were identified. The most contentious issue was the secure room, on which the original three stances taken were characterized by statements such as 'Keep it, we need it', 'Abolish it', 'Change it to a time-out room'. The conflict was resolved eventually, the outcome being a recommendation for significant upgrading of the secure room, to make it more like a time-out space rather than a place for punishment. The most positive features, 'things we like and want to keep', were the outside natural features, especially the sand dunes and stream. Recreational pursuits and sites, e.g woodwork, metalwork, the gymnasium, swimming pool and sports fields, were the next most popular aspects.

The approach used at the residential school was assessed by senior managers, who judged it a success in terms of gaining 'better' information in less time than usual; setting priorities, which in turn helps with decision-making about what to change; being 'therapeutic' and having public relations value; helping people gain understanding and sympathy for the needs of others, as well as building support at operational and organizational levels. Other commentators described the process as relevant and useful, but also fragile in its dependence on unorthodox work that was unfamiliar. It had been 'therapeutic for all the various users who became familiar with each other's views, attitudes, feelings and intentions'. It provided 'useful briefing information for design proposals' and 'there would have been no prospect of obtaining the information by the normal briefing process, and certainly not in the same time'. They also commented on how, by focusing on the building, the potential for confrontation and dissent was reduced. For instance, the tensions surrounding the issue of the secure room were strong and potentially destructive. By allowing the building to be the focus of attention personality clashes were largely avoided and the issue defused and eventually resolved by consensus. If issues remain hidden or unresolved, they are built in, knowingly or unknowingly, to any building or organizational response. If they are addressed openly, there is a good chance that they can be resolved before commitments are made.

Case 9   Developing knowledge – revision of a design code for a fire service

A series of evaluations were carried out on a number of fire stations throughout the country. While there have been short-term benefits, both physical and social, for the users at each of the fire stations evaluated, the prime purpose of the evaluations was to analyse the design procedures that gave rise to the stations and to

Figure 4.19 *A facilitator discusses floor drain problems with fire fighters.*

revise the service's 'Fire Station Design Code'. The evaluations were carried out by the generic evaluation process (Figure 4.19). At review meetings participant groups were asked to make recommendations not only about 'this facility' but also about 'future facilities', and specifically to make recommendations about the design of new fire stations.

As a case in point, a volunteer fire fighter gave the following account of being on call early in a morning: 'You arrive at the station. . . make your way to the lockers. . . oh! the lockers, what a joke. . . let me show you what happens here. . . you search around for your key to your locker suspecting the permanents are playing games with you. . . find the key. . . open up the door. . . at this time your mates are clambering in. . . can't get past your open door. . . almost knock you over as you're pulling on your boots. . . this bench is also in the way. . . who oh earth thought of putting it there? It's OK for the permanents but not for us. . .'

Recommendations drawn from this experience listed modifica-
.ons needed to the layout of the locker room. These have been
implemented and have proved successful. The recommendations
and design modifications have since been incorporated into the
Service's design code. Reports from the evaluations were prepared
in a format agreed by the Fire Service. The format consisted of a
discussion of the various interrelated design issues raised,
followed by a list of recommendations arranged to match headings
used in the Fire Services Design Code. For the building owners,
the Fire Service, the evaluations not only suggested revisions to the
design code but also provided possible explanations as to why
some difficulties in the design of fire stations existed and persisted.
The evaluations have added significantly to the Service's corporate
knowledge.

The case studies we have selected all demonstrate that most people
are quite capable of undertaking planning and early design tasks,
as well as evaluating buildings they use. They can provide answers
to some of the most difficult questions about the relationships of
people, organizations and buildings. The people who are experts
about kitchens are the cooks, but cooks can tell about more than
just cooking. In their domain they can tell about the behaviour of
people who eat, or line up to collect food, and about the
relationships between cooking and eating, kitchen and dining
room, environment and behaviour. We all have expertise in our
own areas of interest. But we can only contribute it if asked, and
the information is of value only when listened to and acted upon.
We believe participatory evaluation is possibly the best tool
available to ensure there are benefits for all interests in a building
when issues of briefing and design, selecting, fixing and
refurbishing buildings are to be addressed. In Chapter 5 we explain
in some detail how to facilitate an evaluation by means of the
generic process.

5

Facilitating evaluations

This chapter is for facilitators; it contains a 'how to' guide to planning and managing an evaluation. It will be of interest to people who want to facilitate evaluations or those, such as managers, who need to understand the tasks and activities of facilitators. We concentrate on the core on-site activities of the evaluation process – introductory meeting, touring interview and review meeting.

An evaluation normally needs two or three facilitators. Their tasks include organizing and managing the evaluation, leading the activities on-site, recording and presenting the comments and recommendations of participants, and promoting action as an outcome. Figure 5.1 summarizes the normal sequence of tasks for facilitators, and can be used as a checklist to ensure all tasks are completed. We begin the chapter by discussing how facilitators may be selected and how they can prepare themselves for the tasks ahead. This starts with clarifying the terms of reference of the specific evaluation and its purpose. It is important to feel comfortable with the purpose and scope of, and time available for, the evaluation, and the commitment of the sponsors and management (financial and otherwise) to it and its outcomes. We then describe the preparation work required of facilitators once they have agreed to go ahead. We focus on the tasks of the core generic elements of the evaluation process. Each task description explains what to do, and adds comment or illustration as further clarification.

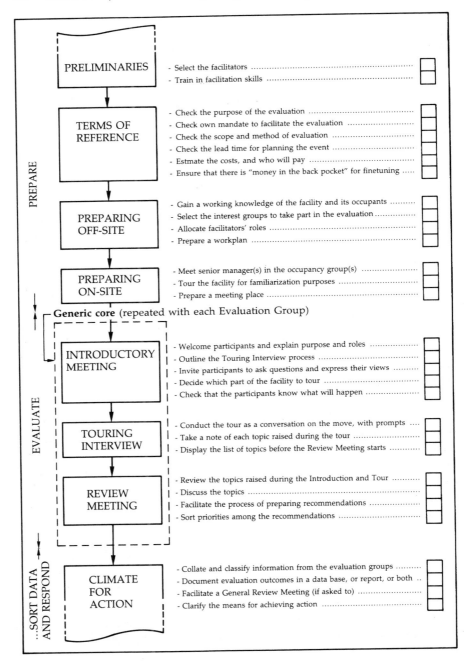

PRELIMINARIES
- Select the facilitators ....
- Train in facilitation skills ....

TERMS OF REFERENCE
- Check the purpose of the evaluation ....
- Check own mandate to facilitate the evaluation ....
- Check the scope and method of evaluation ....
- Check the lead time for planning the event ....
- Estmate the costs, and who will pay ....
- Ensure that there is "money in the back pocket" for finetuning .....

PREPARING OFF-SITE
- Gain a working knowledge of the facility and its occupants ....
- Select the interest groups to take part in the evaluation ....
- Allocate facilitators' roles ....
- Prepare a workplan ....

PREPARING ON-SITE
- Meet senior manager(s) in the occupancy group(s) ....
- Tour the facility for familiarization purposes ....
- Prepare a meeting place ....

Generic core (repeated with each Evaluation Group)

INTRODUCTORY MEETING
- Welcome participants and explain purpose and roles ....
- Outline the Touring Interview process ....
- Invite participants to ask questions and express their views ....
- Decide which part of the facility to tour ....
- Check that the participants know what will happen ....

TOURING INTERVIEW
- Conduct the tour as a conversation on the move, with prompts ....
- Take a note of each topic raised during the tour ....
- Display the list of topics before the Review Meeting starts ....

REVIEW MEETING
- Review the topics raised during the Introduction and Tour ....
- Discuss the topics ....
- Facilitate the process of preparing recommendations ....
- Sort priorities among the recommendations ....

CLIMATE FOR ACTION
- Collate and classify information from the evaluation groups ....
- Document evaluation outcomes in a data base, or report, or both ..
- Facilitate a General Review Meeting (if asked to) ....
- Clarify the means for achieving action ....

PREPARE

EVALUATE

...SORT DATA AND RESPOND

Figure 5.1 *Facilitation tasks.*

Preliminaries

Select the facilitators

Facilitators are normally chosen by the managers who authorize the evaluation. The case studies in Chapter 4 show how the evaluation process can be used in a number of contexts for a variety of purposes. Purpose and context are the main forces that determine the specific way in which the process is applied. They also influence who should facilitate the activity. Every context is different and the choice of facilitators will respond to that difference; however, in principle, the main criterion for their selection is a general confidence that they can successfully carry out the tasks required of them in the specific context and for the agreed purpose. Facilitators should understand and feel comfortable about the evaluation process and their predominantly neutral role in it. They must be clear that it is not they but the participants who evaluate the facility and make recommendations about it.

Facilitators may have an interest in the building or be remote from it. They may have skills related to building use, design or management, but they need not. However, generally we promote the idea of the 'informed facilitator', or facilitation group, who has some understanding of the language of the two major cultures involved in the evaluation – the users and providers. Some or all of them may have done an evaluation before. We find having at least one facilitator who is familiar with the evaluation process is always useful. We also find it helpful if at least one facilitator has knowledge of the building and the occupant organization or organizations; such knowledge not only assists liaison with the various interests in the building in the preparatory stages of the evaluation but can also help clarify issues and comments made during the evaluation itself.

In addition to some knowledge of the evaluation process, and the building and organizations in it, facilitators need particular attitudinal and communication skills. These are primarily listening skills and an ability to suppress temporarily personal and professional values. Facilitation skills develop with experience. They are learned through practice and work on evaluations. Against the argument for 'specializing' facilitation skills is the desire that 'expertise' remains with the participants, and that part of the essential character of the evaluation process is to allow ordinary people to have their say. Too expert or slick facilitation can be off-putting to participants who may be uncertain, naive, not used to being listened to. On the other hand, skilful facilitation can assist participant groups who know what should be done about an issue but not how.

Training in facilitation skills

To assist facilitators we have designed short training sessions, supported by guidance documents. The training sessions concentrate on the activities and attitudes required to conduct successful evaluations, with role plays of the principal events. This chapter summarizes the knowledge we have gained from those activities. We therefore suggest that in preparing for an evaluation facilitators should:

1 Read this chapter fully and use the checklist of evaluation activities to become familiar with the evaluation tasks.
2 Read (again) Chapters 3 and 4, to help clarify the purpose of the specific evaluation and the context for use of the generic process.
3 Conduct a small role play of the three principal activities of the evaluation event – introduction, touring interview, review. To do this, form a small participant group from colleagues. Go through the principal activities but only visit one or two spaces familiar to them. Try to frame one or two recommendations from the limited range of issues raised. A mock-up evaluation, which can be completed in half an hour, provides good insight into the nature of the whole evaluation event.

Terms of reference

Facilitators should be clear about the terms of reference before agreeing to undertake an evaluation. The terms of reference should cover matters of purpose, mandate, scope, methods of evaluation, lead time, costs and assurance from management that there is 'money in the back pocket' for finetuning the facility.

Check the purpose of the evaluation and the facilitators' mandate

Evaluations have many purposes. Check who has asked for the evaluation and why it is wanted. On whose authority? What are the expected outcomes and benefits to the people who will take part? Evaluations should be needed, asked for, useful. It is important to be clear about their purpose, so that they can be designed to fit the circumstances. Address the goals and concerns of all those who will be taking part. There must be 'something in it' for everyone. No matter what the underlying purpose, an evaluation must be worth doing in some way for everyone; otherwise there is unlikely to be the necessary co-operation and collaboration. When an evaluation is proposed, it is worthwhile considering the concerns and values of all those with interests in the building. Will their interests be addressed?

There is a degree of choice in most aspects of planning an evaluation. As we have seen, the process can be combined with other participatory and collaborative design and management activities to serve a range of purposes, including fixing and selecting accommodation, assisting briefing and design and, as we will discuss more fully in Chapter 6, to develop corporate knowledge. However, while the context varies, the core activities of introduction, touring interview and review are consistent, although, as we have shown in Case studies 4 and 5, there can be some flexibility as to the timing and order of their use.

In addition, facilitators should be prepared to be flexible during an evaluation. For instance, on the fine-tuning evaluation of an office building one of the participant groups had already met together before coming to the evaluation event. They presented a list of the issues they wanted to discuss. They felt there was no need to go on a touring interview. The facilitators' response was to say OK. They then effectively merged the introduction direct into the review. However, during the review the group did move out of the meeting room to have illustrated in two different rooms specific points at issue. This is a normal part of a touring interview. Furthermore, as spaces representative of the range used in the building were not being visited, the facilitators ensured that some reference was made to them in conversation. Thus while the concerns of the particular participant group were given priority, their more general perceptions were also elicited. The essential functions of the touring interview – raising issues, illustrating them and bringing them forward for discussion at the review – were retained.

Check the scope and method of the evaluation

Is using the generic process appropriate for the purpose and context of the issues being addressed? Consider the objectives of the evaluation. Try to summarize these concisely. This usually helps determine the specific approach to be adopted. The generic process offers advantages where issues concerning people and buildings are important. It is exploratory. It may bring to light important issues that were not previously known about, or were known only to the groups who experienced them rather than those who could do something about them. Focused evaluations tend to gather precise information, which can support detailed analysis. As we have suggested, exploratory evaluations can be used as preparation for a focused evaluation. We recommend strongly that an exploratory evaluation should always precede one at the focused level.

Check the lead time for planning the event

We usually plan a lead time of at least a month for preparation of an evaluation event. Four days is the maximum time we have needed on-site to evaluate a large facility with many participant groups. This is based on the normal time taken for an introduction, touring interview and review of 2 to 2½ hours for each participant group. The general review, attended by all the participants in the initial evaluation event and any other people with interests in the building or the evaluation outcomes, is normally planned for no more than 4 weeks after the evaluation event. So, about 2 to 2½ months is the normal time frame for completing most evaluation activities. Reporting of the activities is held within those times, but resulting action often occurs later.

In larger buildings with significant numbers of staff enough time must be given to the evaluation event to ensure that issues are considered comprehensively. Sometimes there has been concern about the 4-day length of the event. There is potential for essentially the same information to be repeated by the different participant groups, and certainly some similarity of comment does occur. However, the number of times an issue is referred to by different participants is a useful indication of its importance. It is also important that facilitators remain sensitive to the different nuances of comments about the same topic, as they may inform the process of developing recommendations. As we have shown, shorter evaluations are possible in some circumstances, e.g. in buildings with a small population. Where evaluation events are to be on an annual or biennial basis, consideration should be given to possible ways of condensing them.

Estimate the costs, and who will pay

Evaluations can cost as much or as little as you, or your organization, can afford. Generally, since the benefits are shared, so are the direct costs. However, there are immediate costs that have to be met, and there are costs resulting from the evaluation. Who is paying the costs and how that is to be paid must be determined at an early stage. The person-hours to be spent on evaluation can be readily assessed, and guesstimates made of whether anyone will expect or require payment for attending the evaluation. Establish a means for monitoring expenditure. Evaluation events with which we have been connected have cost somewhere between £2000 and £5000 to conduct, depending on the length of the evaluation and who is facilitating it. These figures do not include costings of the wages and salaries of in-house staff in participant groups. They are based on a charge-out rate for facilitators (where payment is required), allowances for transport, report publication and sundries, and for payments to one or two participant group members outside the organizations principally concerned.

Ensure that there is 'money in the back pocket' for fine-tuning

Some recommendations arising from the evaluation will improve the building being evaluated. There must therefore be the mandate and the money for something significant and obvious to happen as a result of an evaluation event, otherwise there can be serious social damage as people wonder what it was all about and why they bothered taking part. Their prejudices are confirmed or reinforced. There is little point in going ahead with an evaluation if no action results. Adequate resources, 'money in the back pocket', are essential to implement at least some of the recommendations and to keep staff informed of progress, especially where action is delayed or not possible. Funds can often be made available from a variety of sources – the client/building owner, the tenant organization, minor capital works, maintenance votes, or as one-off allocation.

In our experience 'money in the back pocket', for immediate fine-tuning items, has rarely exceeded £20,000 in major facilities. This is in addition to the costs of the evaluation event. Thus, in the most general terms, evaluations and the resulting fine-tuning can be carried out for something less than 1 per cent of the initial capital cost of a building, and more commonly for considerably less. The costs are minor in comparison with the capital and operating costs, and negligible compared to salary costs. Those who take part in evaluations very often report that the benefits exceed their expectations and cost nothing. At the previously mentioned office building where the building liaison managers agreed to meet monthly the costs were minimal and led to savings through better management.

Once you have agreed to be a facilitator and to the terms of reference for the specific evaluation, you can begin preparing for the evaluation.

Preparing off-site

Gain a working knowledge of the building and its occupants

You need to know about the building and its occupancy to plan the evaluation. One or more of your facilitation group may be familiar with the building or the organization and can take a key role in informing the others. People in the building and organization and archived documents can provide further information. Who are the present occupants? What is the history of occupancy? When was the building constructed? Is the original brief available? What drawings and specifications are available? Find out if any technical reports or previous evaluations have been done. Preparing a brief background of a building helps you become knowledgeable about it, and can also form a basis for any reporting of the evaluation. A summary description may contain:

1 A summary of the 'background' of the project – major events, dates, decisions, costs and people.
2 Diagrammatic plans/layout of the building and site.
3 A brief written description of the facility, its physical provisions and how it is operated.

Select the interest groups to take part in the evaluation

What interest groups in the building can you identify? Ideally all interests should be represented. Some recurring interests are:

Occupants	Designers	Cleaners
Managers	Builders	Suppliers
Visitors	Consultants	Insurance agents
Owners	Maintenance staff	Financiers

List the interests specific to the building to be evaluated. Are there distinct 'sub-interests' in large groups, such as 'support staff' and 'managers' as subsets of 'occupants'? Representatives should be able to speak for other people in the interest group from which they are drawn. Non-participants can pass on their comments about the building to the relevant representatives before the evaluation. In some evaluations people have come to the evaluation with a list of comments from others in the same interest group. This is fine.

We have found that five to ten participant groups are usually enough to represent the interests in a facility. Groups should have no more than three to seven people in them, or they become difficult to manage as a single group. For example, the larger the group, the more difficult it is to keep everyone together during the touring interview so that each person can hear what the others have to say. The number of people associated with a building and the range of interests in it will influence the number and composition of participant groups. A relatively large population of occupants may call for two, three or more participant groups, yet a group of three maintenance personnel may represent the entire population of maintenance staff. Seek advice in selecting representatives or delegate the task to a person with first-hand knowledge of the interest in question. This can widen the group of people with interest in the evaluation effort. Prepare a full list of proposed representatives before formally inviting them. Make sure each participant receives a personal invitation to attend the evaluation event. Some refusals may occur, so obtain acknowledgements so that alternative arrangements can be made in the event that someone cannot attend. At least one facilitator should be available in the weeks before the evaluation to answer participant and management questions.

There are two approaches to deciding on the individuals who will make up the participant groups. There can be homogeneous participant groups (all members of a group representing a similar interest) or heterogeneous groups (different people in the same group with different interests). The former tend to focus discussion on concerns of mutual interest. The latter provide different viewpoints, which can stimulate discussion. We suggest that

HOMOGENEOUS GROUPS	Each group is composed of people with similar experiences with the facility and similar interests and values. Discussions tend to be harmonious and convergent. People speak freely, 'within these walls...' Minimal attitude change with respect to other groups, and no opportunity (during the evaluation) to negotiate. Process requires only basic facilitation skills.
HETEROGENEOUS GROUPS	Each group is composed of people with different experiences with the facility and at least some different interests and values. Discussions tend to be constrained. People with power tend to dominate. When differences become explicit, this can lead to conflict, position-taking, or both. Opportunity for negotiation, increased understanding, compromise agreement and changes in attitude. Process requires advanced facilitation skills.

Figure 5.2 *Generic options for the composition of participant groups.*

unless you have experience of evaluations or similar participatory activities, you will find it easier to work with homogeneous participant groups. In other words, if you have 'entry level' facilitation skills, work with homogeneous groups (Figure 5.2). We find participants generally feel more comfortable speaking in a group with similar interests. Heterogeneous groups have more complex dynamics, can be difficult to focus, even confrontational, and are therefore more difficult for facilitators to deal with.

For instance, in one of our trial evaluations a barracks corporal was part of a management group which included the commanding officer and three other commissioned officers. In the laundry area he was seen shaking his head about various comments by the officers about the use of washing machines (Figure 5.3) but he did not speak. There had been problems with the domestic machines regularly breaking down. The men wanted small industrial machines, at no greater expense. Later we invited the corporal to join a participant group with other barrack corporals, and he spoke freely about his reservations with the officers' comments. What the officers' didn't know was that while the domestic machines could cope with clothes, the soldiers returning exhausted from exercises would throw everything including their boots into the machines (it was also the best way to get the last bits of mud off the boots). However, when this was explained to the major at a general review, he agreed that industrial machines could replace the domestic when they were beyond repair. While military hierarchies may not exist explicitly in the civilian world, we take some trouble to ensure as best we can that no one will feel inhibited before inviting participants. We want everyone to feel they can speak their mind freely.

It is often necessary to use heterogeneous groups, especially on buildings with small populations. It is important to be confident that groups with mixed interests do not inhibit individual contributions. Be aware of and moderate where possible the potential conflicts of status and authority. As your skills develop, you may feel more confident about working with heterogeneous groups. Whatever the composition of groups, opportunity should be given at some point in an evaluation for all participants to come together and for the viewpoints and recommendations of the various interest groups to be compared and discussed. General review meetings always consist of a large heterogenous group, and require confident facilitation because of the large number of people present.

Figure 5.3 *The major speaks out. The corporal standing behind the major did not agree with what his superior officer and the other officers were saying about the laundry facilities, but he was not prepared to voice his disagreement in this situation.*

Allocate facilitators' roles

Facilitation leadership may be assigned to one person, or taken in turn with each participant group evaluation. The principal facilitation tasks are managing the evaluation, explaining its purpose and procedures, guiding participants through the touring interview and review meeting, and helping negotiate recommendations. It is also important that someone 'mops up' any comments, ensuring that the participant group remains coherent throughout the evaluation, and keeps the evaluation to time. Decide who will do what. To what extent and for what purpose will you need to take photographs or measurements? Will you use photographs for recording and reporting purposes or slides for the presentation of issues at a general review meeting? What documentation and equipment will you need? Will you use prompts, checklists or questionnaires to assist or complement the principal data gathering of the touring interview?

Prepare a workplan

Review what has to be done before and after the evaluation. Check evaluation activities and their durations. Check:

1 The date for the evaluation activity at least 3 to 4 weeks in advance.
2 The total duration of the introduction (½ hour), touring interview (1 hour) and review activities (1–1½ hours).
3 Access to the building spaces, hours of operation of the building, including meal times, tea/coffee breaks, shifts, etc.
4 That a room in the building can be made available to you as your meeting base on-site.
5 That all documentation required can be available in time.
6 Budget for fees and payments (if any) to people attending are settled.

Evaluation activities are potentially disruptive to the day to day operations in the building to be evaluated though in practice disruption is minimal. Keep management fully informed of the agenda. Arrange that other occupants not playing a part in the evaluation are informed about what is going on.

You are now ready to move on-site and begin the events that are the core of the evaluation process.

Preparing on-site

Meet senior manager(s) in the occupancy group(s)

The first thing to do on arriving at the building is to meet management, introduce yourselves and check that the programme arrangements are in order. Check that they understand the purpose and benefits of the visit. If they are convinced of the benefits, they will insist on ensuring the evaluation proceeds smoothly.

Tour the facility

If you are unfamiliar with the building, take a tour. You can check the building's physical layout and where people are located. You can also check the accuracy of the building plans. You need to be familiar with the building so that you can assist participants to plan their touring interview routes.

Prepare a meeting place

A room must be set aside in the building as the base from which to work. The introduction and review meetings with each group of participants will be held there. The room should have:

- A whiteboard, blackboard or large flipchart in easy view of participants.
- Wall space for up to ten large sheets of paper.
- Comfortable chairs arranged in a semicircle so that people can see each other.
- Shelves or table(s) to hold materials and equipment used by the task group.

The room should be secure when left unattended during the touring interviews. It needs to be well but not too strongly lit,

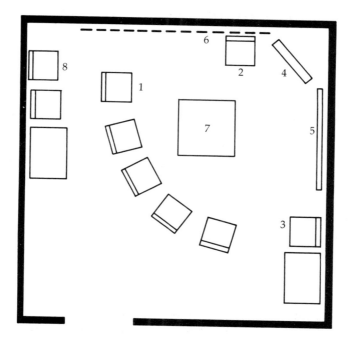

KEY

1 Chairs for group members (participants).
2 Facilitator.
3 Note-maker/facilitator.
4 Flipchart (or screen with copying capability).
5 Whiteboard.
6 Wall space.
7 Table (preferably low).
8 Spare furniture + 3rd facilitator + coffee.

Figure 5.4 *Room layout suitable for introductory and review meetings.*

well-ventilated and reasonably quiet (Figure 5.4). When ready, you can begin the evaluation with the first participant group.

Note that the activities of introduction, touring interview and review meeting are repeated with each participant group as many times as there are groups.

The generic process: introductory meeting

Welcome participants and explain purpose and roles

Welcome the participants and introduce yourselves. Ask participants to introduce themselves. Ask them to outline their interest in the building and what they do or have done to support their interest. Prompt questions include the following. 'What do you do here?' 'When did you first work in/visit/become involved with the facility?' Describe the proposed agenda for their evaluation, then explain that the general aim of the evaluation is to learn from the experiences of people with different points of view, and that their role as participants is to evaluate the facility and make recommendations about it. Make sure they understand that you will keep notes on individual comments made during the touring interview, so that they can be brought forward as the bases for discussion at the review. The only information that is recorded from the evaluation for use later is the recommendation statements agreed by each participant group. If parts of the evaluation are to be photographed, explain the purpose and use of the photographs, and check that none of the participants object. Answer questions as they arise.

Outline the 'touring interview' process

The tour is a memory-jogging exercise to help the group remember topics that are important to them. Remind each group of participants that the review to follow is where topics will be discussed in full and recommendations made. Explain that other groups will be doing their evaluations independently but in a similar manner. Tell them who the other groups are and that all findings will be made available to all groups. If a general review meeting is to be held, state its purpose and where and when it will take place. Explanation of the process can be aided by flipcharts. Displaying ideas in front of everyone ensures the same thing is communicated to everyone. It also provides a way for individuals to check their understanding or verify an idea (Figure 5.5).

Figure 5.5 *An introductory meeting in progress.*

Invite participants to ask questions and express their views

Invite questions about the purpose or process. Questions may include the following. 'Why a participatory evaluation?' 'Who will use the information?' 'How do we know that our recommendations will make any difference?' 'Can I tell you about opinions and experiences of some of the others I work with?' It is quite common for participants to come to the evaluation event to speak about or list topics they or their immediate colleagues feel merit attention. Some participants may have canvassed views quite widely. Let people have their say. For instance, we have had groups arrive with fully typed reports. We have had individuals arrive with their colleagues' views jotted down on scraps of paper. If topics are brought to the introductory meeting, whatever their form, written or verbal, from participants or others, record the topics and display them as keywords or phrases on a flipchart or the whiteboard. Make sure participants understand that all topics raised will be fully discussed at the review meeting. While accepting some discussion, suggest that these topics be held for explanation during the touring interview and further discussion at the review meeting to follow. Seek the group's view on how some of the topics raised might affect the proposed agenda and tour. It is important to be flexible at this stage about these matters, as you will want to make it clear to participants that you are listening to what they want to say and are prepared to accommodate their wishes.

Decide which parts of the facility to tour

Before starting the tour, discuss the route to be taken. Stress that the tour 'belongs' to the participants and that they should take the tour wherever they think it should go to point out or illustrate good and bad features of the facility or its operation. Groups that have an interest in the facility as a whole may elect to tour parts that are representative of the facility as a whole, such as a sample of 'typical' office floors in a multi-storey office building. Although the same spaces will often be visited by all participants, others may be of particular interest to particular participants, such as the service areas under the control of the service engineers. Suggest a route that includes a representative set of spaces inside and outside the building. Let participants make suggestions and alterations. While not all spaces need be visited, it is good to visit a representative sample. The comments of participants who may have only a passing knowledge of what a space is used for or how it is used can often be pertinent. Explain this to each group.

Check that participants know what will happen

Check before leaving the introduction that participants:

1 Are happy about the route to be followed.
2 Know what will happen in each space visited.
3 Understand that comments will be recorded only in summary form as a reminder service for the review meeting to follow.

4 Are aware that photographs or measurements of things commented on as the tour progresses may be taken or noted for recording later.

The generic process: touring interview

Conduct the tour as a conversation on the move, with prompts

Begin the tour by moving as a group to the first space on the agreed route (Figure 5.6). Let participants talk about whatever they perceive to be important about the place. Listen and probe but do not lay down what topics are to be discussed or the direction that the discussion should take. Prompts should be directed towards finding out aspects that 'work well', not just the problems, and to identify operational, social and organizational concerns, not only physical features of the building. The building is often a convenient scapegoat for organizational problems. Where personal

Figure 5.6 *A touring interview.*

or personnel problems exist, 'blaming' the building can be a convenient means of saving face or avoiding embarrassment.

Avoid asking leading or loaded questions, such as, 'Do you like the colour scheme?', or even, 'What do you think of the decor?' Use such questions as 'What happens here?'; 'What is important about this space?'; 'What works well . . . what would you have done again . . . and why?'; 'Why is that important?'; 'Can you explain that/tell me more?'; 'How do you feel about that?'; 'If you could change things, what would you do? . . . if only one thing?' Such questions allow participants to respond in their own words about things important to them.

Take a note of each topic raised during the tour

Note the topics raised by participants. A sample page of field notes is shown in Figure 5.7. A 'topic' is any subject or theme that arises during the discussion, usually as a result of direct observation of a part of the facility or in comments made when talking about the facility. Be accurate and avoid making interpretations. If unclear, then ask for further explanation, or if something is lacking, ask for it to be repeated. It is reasonably important, but not vital, that all topics raised by the participants are heard and noted down. So the facilitators must work to keep the group together and limit concurrent subgroup discussions. It is all right to be seen recording, as it assures participants their ideas are being taken seriously. A few keywords or phrases – image, height of switches, ventilation system, signposting – can be noted as a further reminder of the essence of what was commented on, and can be used as a 'memory bank' to be brought forward at the review meeting. A photograph can be taken or a note to take a photo later can also be made. It is important that participants are given time to warm to the event and for them to give full comment in each space. Repeat the prompt questions in each space visited on the touring interview. Make sure there is enough time spent in each space that participants feel all the relevant issues have been raised before moving on. However, it is also important not to shorten the time available for the review meeting, in which issues will be discussed again, with the view to forming recommendations for action.

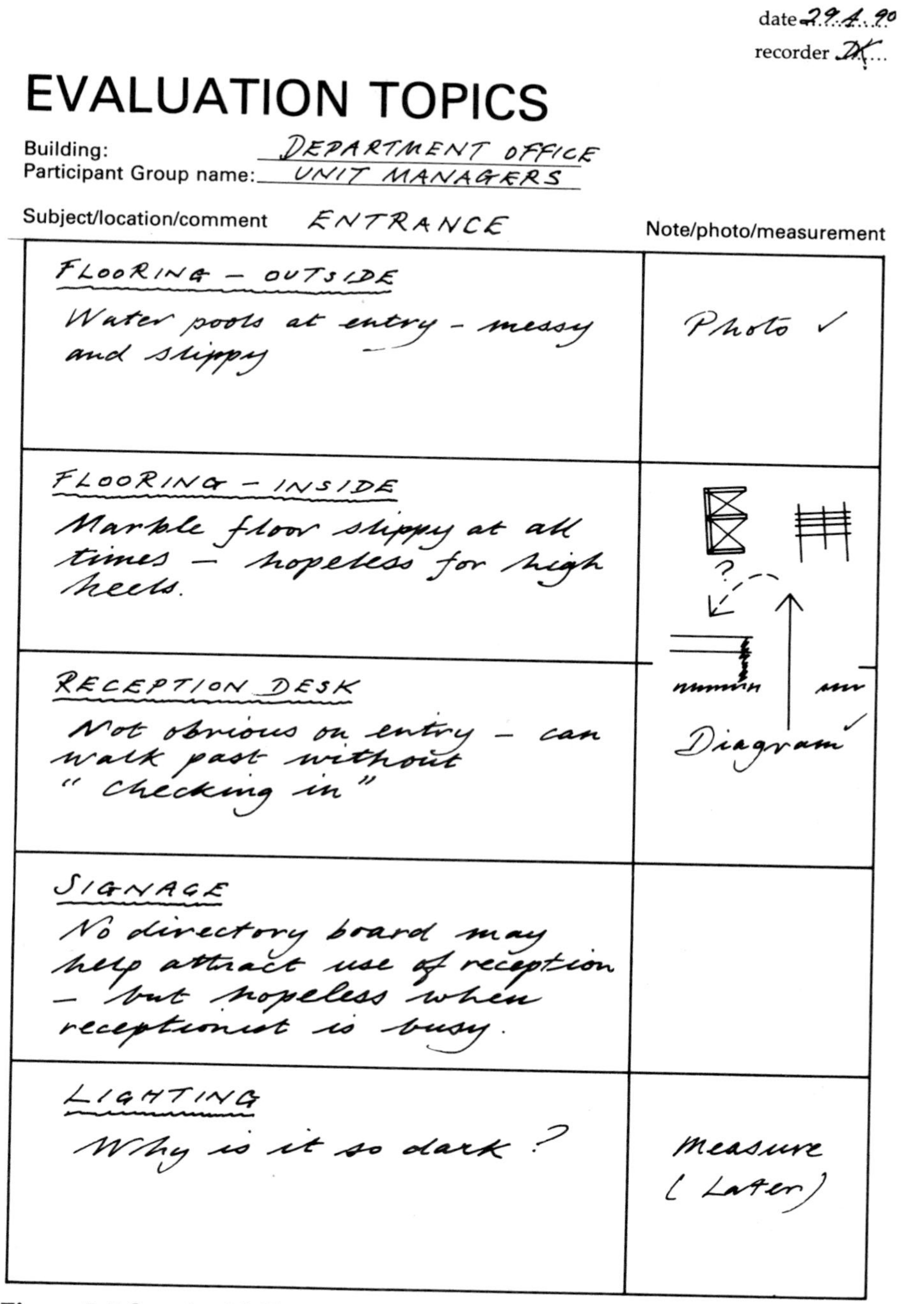

date 29.4.90
recorder DK

EVALUATION TOPICS

Building: _DEPARTMENT OFFICE_
Participant Group name: _UNIT MANAGERS_

Subject/location/comment   _ENTRANCE_   Note/photo/measurement

FLOORING — OUTSIDE Water pools at entry – messy and slippy	Photo ✓
FLOORING — INSIDE Marble floor slippy at all times — hopeless for high heels.	
RECEPTION DESK Not obvious on entry – can walk past without " checking in "	Diagram
SIGNAGE No directory board may help attract use of reception — but hopeless when receptionist is busy.	
LIGHTING Why is it so dark ?	Measure (Later)

Figure 5.7 *Sample of field notes recording some of the topics raised by the participant group.*

Display the list of topics before the review meeting starts

Some minutes before the end of the tour (or during a coffee break) a facilitator should return to the meeting room to print the list of topics on a whiteboard or more flipchart pages. This may mean adding to topics already raised at the introduction. Display them in the meeting room in readiness for the group to work with. The list is a menu to which the group members can add as they see fit, and from which they select topics on which to make recommendations.

Once interviews have been conducted in all the spaces agreed for the tour, the group returns to the meeting room for the review meeting.

The generic process: review meeting

Review the topics raised during the introduction and touring interview

Go through the topics recorded during the introductory meeting and the touring interview, inviting any corrections or additions to the list. Some topics will be repeated or be very similar. With the group's agreement, these can be combined. Others may be too vague or very broad in scope; these need to be made more explicit or divided into more detailed topics. Record all this on the whiteboard or flipchart sheets, so that all members can see the complete list of topics that the group has agreed are important to them (Figure 5.8). The list should be retained for transcription for reporting purposes.

Discuss the topics

Spend some time letting the group freely discuss the topics. Watch for areas of misunderstanding or disagreement, and work to resolve differences where this can be done in a few minutes. Ask such questions as the following. 'What have you noticed that makes you say that?' 'Does everyone see it that way . . . are there other points of view about this?' 'Can we find out why there seem to be different angles on this?' 'What are the facts as we see them?'

Figure 5.8 *A review meeting.*

'Help me understand the cause for that.' Not all topics need to be discussed in detail. Comments about topics that are developed in discussion are written up on the whiteboard or flipcharts as the discussion progresses, by one or more of the facilitators. Placing a clear description of the issues of a topic in front of participants aids understanding about its precise nature, which in turn assists the development of recommendations for action about the topic.

Facilitate the process of preparing recommendations

To begin the process of writing recommendations, ask the group to select one topic that they agree is very important to them, or to agree the priority of issues to be discussed. Dealing with each issue in turn, ask the participants to formulate a concise statement summing up their observation on the matter and any recommendation(s) they may wish to make. This is essentially a continuation of the discussion, but enables the facilitator to begin to move the conversation towards recommendations for action. Write these statements on flipcharts or board so that the wording can be progressively adjusted until consensus is reached (Figure 5.8).

Don't rush ratification of either statements or recommendations. Be prepared to adjust and amend both on the flipchart or board until they have been fully discussed and agreed to by all. 'Agreement to differ' or 'minority recommendations' are acceptable where consensus is not possible. Minority recommendations should be recorded as such. When framing recommendations, encourage expression in a positive mode. The recommendations are intended to promote action. They should be stated in terms that make the action clear. Recommendations should begin with a verb, such as 'install', 'replace', 'investigate'. For instance, here are two sample recommendations from a fine-tuning evaluation of an office building:

- *Space equity*
  (Senior management to) review policy on space allocations by section and unit. Consider use of private and shared space, especially meeting rooms. Unit managers should consult and negotiate with staff and make submissions within 21 days. Senior staff to communicate intended actions within further 7 days.

- *Slipping at entrance*
  Seek specialist advice to find ways of reducing the likelihood of people slipping at the main entrance (internally and externally).

A participant group can be expected to generate eight to fifteen recommendations.

Repeat the procedure with each topic until the participants are content that they have dealt with the main points in their evaluation. The first few topics may take a relatively long time to complete as participants learn to reach consensus and make their recommendations explicit. Sometimes recommendations 'fall out' quite readily, are simply developed and agreed quickly. Other topics may require more than one recommendation for the group to feel the issues have been addressed fully. This can take time.

Sort priorities among the recommendations

The last activity of the review meeting is to settle the priority or relative importance of each recommendation. There are several ways to manage this. One is to 'give' each participant an equal number of A, B and C rankings and ask them to assign all their rankings to the complete set of recommendations. These rankings are recorded on the whiteboard or flipcharts. Where an electronic whiteboard has been available, it is possible for all participants to leave their review meeting with a copy of their group's recommendations. To wind up the review meeting, thank the participant group for its co-operation and contribution to the evaluation. The members will want to know what will happen with their recommendations. Reiterate the time and place for the general review meeting, if there is to be one, and the agreed procedures for communicating and actioning the recommendations.

Collate all information

If possible after each review meeting, ensure that all relevant information has been gathered and recorded. Transcribe and classify recommendations; take photographs and measurements as required. Each recommendation should be identified by a keyword or key phrase to help collation, analysis and reporting. If it is not possible to complete the task of transcribing and classifying recommendations after each review, make sure it is done before the end of each working day. Remember, by the end of the evaluation event you will have about 100 recommendation statements.

Measurements and photographs of specific aspects of the facility that have been the subject of recommendations by the participant groups should also be recorded before leaving the site. This provides quantitative data and graphic illustration to supplement the judgements of the participants.

There are now a number of activities that occur off-site. They may be carried out as part of a reporting procedure or in preparation for a general review meeting, or both. These activities are all intended to promote action in response to the recommendations of the participants in the evaluation.

Create a climate for action

Collate and classify information

It is good practice to produce some record of the evaluation. A report can be used to assure participants that their recommendations have been accurately recorded and to see the recommendations of other participants. It is important to include all recommendations in a report. Don't record all the comments. It is better to record only comments that did not lead to recommendations. Such comments are often references to what is good in the building, not requiring any remedial or short-term action. They are nevertheless important to record, as they may have an impact on longer-term action, like the briefing of similar facilities.

Document evaluation outcomes in a database or report, or both

A report can be used as the basis for further negotiation with building management about action in response to the recommendations. If a report is produced, including the following information may aid consistency of format:

1 A cover sheet.
2 A contents list.
3 Summary of evaluation method.
4 A brief background to the building project.
5 A photographic, drawn and written description of the building.
6 All the recommendations, including those of the facilitators, if appropriate, with their associated keywords and phrases.
7 Photographs where appropriate to illustrate recommendations or particular issues.

Collation and analysis activities already carried out should reduce the time required to complete this task. The least demanding procedure is to publish copies or photo-reductions of each of the participant-group recommendations as recorded at the review meetings. A listing by keyword of the subjects of each recommendation is useful. The list should identify which and how many participant groups made recommendations on any particular subject. It should also indicate the priority ranking individuals gave that subject (see Table 5.1). This helps identify the subjects that were of most concern to the participants. Such information is a useful starting point for discussion at general review meetings. A more ambitious reporting exercise might include classifying the recommendations in various ways to serve different audiences and different storage/retrieval procedures. Such an outcome is usually more useful if the individual evaluation event is part of a programme of evaluations.

Occasionally a report with recommendations clearly identified and classified can be sufficient to promote action. Present the report to the sponsor and meet to discuss what action will take place and how information about that will best be disseminated. It is important in these circumstances that part of the agreed action is to inform the participants in the evaluation about what is to happen.

We prefer to hold a general review meeting 3 or 4 weeks after the evaluation event. A general review allows all those concerned to learn of the recommendations of others, to formulate final recommendations for action and to learn what action will be taken. Before such a meeting discuss with appropriate managers the nature of the recommendations and their attitude to implementing them. As we have seen, it is sometimes possible for each recommendation to be tagged with a probable cost estimate, and for statements to be made about what funds could be made available and when. Participants at the general review meeting should be given clear information on real resource and budget limitations. It is our experience that the provision of information about probable financial and resource allocations as they relate to recommendations are dealt with reasonably and realistically in the general forum. Introducing external constraints such as time or finance helps focus such meetings.

The draft report, or at least the recommendations of each participant group, should also be made available to all participants before the general review. By classifying the participant group recommendations under topic headings and inspecting the wording of each recommendation, one can propose a set of 'summary recommendations'. Such summary recommendations should encapsulate the underlying intention or intentions of the recommendations within each topic. The summary recommendations can form part of the report and be circulated for informal

Table 5.1   List of topics raised by twelve participant groups in an evaluation and number of times priorities ranked.

Subject	Groups	1	2	3	4	5
Back light surfaces	B					
Basement doors	B					
Blinds	D G					
Building – colour scheme	H I J					1
Building – general comments	B G I J K L					
Building – location	H					
Building – user guidelines	C					
Cabling – telephones, power, computer	F I K					
Cafeteria – dishwasher	B					
Cafeteria – more inviting	H					
Carpet	A D I					1
Computers	D G K					3
Coping with change	H	1				
Creche	B					
Entrance – main doors	H					
Entrance – reception	A H	1	1	1	1	1
Entrance – slipping at	A B C D E F G H I			3	1	1
Entrance – water hazards	A D H			1		
Equipment – AV equipment	G J					
Equipment – boardroom-booking system	A D F J					
Fax	D					
Feedback	G					
Furniture – provide ergonomic	B K		1			
Gym	B G H					
Layout – space	G H J K L					
Layout – space equity	A B C D E F H	18	6	1	2	1
Layout – unit layout	D J K					
Layout – workstations	B C D E L					
Library	B					
Lifts	J					
Lights	A B D E F G H I L	2	2	2	5	
Loading bay – delivery facilities	A			1		
Maintenance/cleaning	F H I		1	1		2
Meeting rooms	A D J				1	1
Noise	A C D E F G H L	1	3	2	2	4
Office – manager's	E					
Outside areas	H					
Outside spaces – decking	B					
Outside spaces – outside roof	C					
Photocopier – noise/ventilation	A B E G J K					
Privacy – meeting rooms	B D E G H					
Privacy – workstations	C E F G L					
Safety (mandatory required anyway)	F G	1		1		1
Security	B C E G				1	
Sick bay	D					1

Table 5.1 (continued)

Subject	Groups	Priority rank/count				
		1	2	3	4	5
Signage – other areas	B C D E F G H J					1
Reception – signposting/identification	A B G H J		1		1	1
Socialization	F			1		
Staff numbers	G J L					
Storage – cupboards	A G H I L				1	1
Storage – personal	A B E F G H L		1	3	1	
Storage – records	B E F G L					
Storage – stationery management	D					
Storage – workspaces	A B D E F G H J L					
Tea bar – layout	B D E F G J					
Tea bar – facilities and use	A I J				1	2
Telephones – meeting rooms	B G H					
Telephones – other	D E F G H J					
Temperature	C H J L					
Temperature – portable heaters	A					
Toilets	H I J K			1	1	1
Ventilation	A B C D E F G H L	7	12	4	4	1
Ventilation – air quality	B F G H J L			1	1	1
Visitors' needs	C E					

discussion by participants before the general review meeting. They can form a useful basis for discussion and help structure the meeting agenda.

Facilitate a general review meeting

General review meetings bring all participants in the evaluation event together, and any other building users who wish to contribute. The purpose of the meeting is to discuss and negotiate with all participants the recommendations made by each participant group at the evaluation event, to develop with the larger group consensus recommendations, and to prioritize them for action. The meeting follows in principle the format of normal participant group review meetings. The meeting normally lasts no more than 2 hours, which is as long as is practicable to maintain the interest and cohesiveness of an audience of this size. Thus it is useful at the start of the meeting to establish priorities for discussion within the given time frame.

If appropriate, use a short slide presentation to remind participants of the nature of each issue and recommendation. The recommendations of each participant group from the initial event are used as the starting point for discussion. There are a number of ways in which these may be reintroduced to the participants. If 'summary recommendations' have already been made available, then the order of discussion can be agreed from a list of them displayed on a flipchart or overhead transparency. Another approach is to display the recommendations of each participant group around the meeting room on flipcharts for inspection and consideration before and throughout the meeting. The recommendations can again be sorted and categorized to help identify and order topics for discussion.

Help participants discuss and ratify the recommendations and their groupings as presented. Agree an order for the discussion of issues and recommendations. With the larger audience, the negotiation of final agreed recommendations requires considerable skill on the part of the facilitator or facilitators. They must have the confidence to facilitate the meeting effectively. Personal interpretations of recommendations must not be imposed. Throughout the process you must ensure the meeting is not taken over by any factional interests or the more vocal participants. Finally, ranking techniques may be used again to help everyone present order discussion and determine priorities.

Clarify the means for achieving action

The major outcome of the general review meeting is consensus agreement on the most important recommendations and their priority. If possible, conclude with an explanation of what action will now be taken. If you have been given authority by management to declare action on some recommendations, then make some undertakings for work to be carried out 'on the spot'. Intentions for action in response to other recommendations should also be declared, and the mechanism for keeping staff informed of progress made clear.

Postscript

Where necessary, it is important to establish mechanisms for the ongoing management of responses to the recommendations. A good strategy is to spread the responsibilities to ensure that action is taken because people come and go within an organization. Managers move on and can take with them the commitment to evaluation outcomes. It is important that the commitment is embedded as well as possible in the organization, and not left as the responsibility of a few individuals. It is not easy to maintain the impetus and energy released during the evaluation process, and perhaps it is not necessary to. We notice that users are actually quite modest with their expectations and grateful for improvements. They are happy to have been listened to and to see responses to their efforts. However, it is always important that action results.

So far we have discussed the participatory evaluation of facilities as though those initiating them had the support of other like-minded people. We have assumed that they were in a situation where there was a commitment to working towards a better understanding between the two cultures of users and providers. Yet this may well not be the case. Often the mission statements, management structures, and accounting procedures in organizations, especially large organizations, mitigate against people trying to work in a more cross-cultural way. Large organizations, both user and provider, have special challenges, but also opportunities for those trying to institute practices based on participatory evaluation.

Large organizations, as we have experienced them in New Zealand and Canada, and read in reports from elsewhere, have a hierarchical management structure. They are managed by control from the top, with a chain of command, rules and procedures. Such a structure inherently works against dialogue. A new venture like facility evaluation, if it were to occur at all, would originate from a top-down directive rather than a bottom-up initiative. There will be fears at all levels about the unknown outcomes that an evaluation may uncover, and further challenges will occur over how to pay and who to charge for the evaluation, and who, with the pressure of work, is to be assigned to do it.

Those convinced of the value of undertaking facility evaluations, and of working in a participatory way, have then a difficult and challenging time ahead of them. Initially they have to seek out others in the organization with whom they can collaborate. This does not mean that they necessarily work together or are in the same section of the organization. Rather it means forming an alliance with others with whom a similar interest in dialogue and working in a participatory way is shared, and who value the idea that a facility should fit the way people want to use it. If help can be obtained from people with authority, then they may act as the champions, offering support when asked for, and, if necessary, guidance in ways of working. With such people in an alliance it is possible to reflect on how best to introduce the idea of evaluation, either as a one-off event for a specific purpose or as a longer-term intervention. With their help, it should be possible to negotiate the opportunity to implement what you want to do with those responsible for the decision to commit resources.

What is being negotiated is not only the need for evaluation but also the opportunity to use a participatory method. Where necessary, this may call for many meetings, negotiating with each decision-maker in turn, and possibly even together. Each will have to be convinced of the benefits of adopting a new approach to decision-making about the design and management of the facilities for which they have responsibility. They will need to be persuaded that what happens now is not working. If it is working, why change it? Evidence will be needed. Signs that design and management practices are not effective include:

1 The number and level of complaints registered about a building or how it is run.
2 Evidence of low productivity or morale.
3 Reduced tenancy ratios in the building not otherwise attributable to market conditions.
4 Evidence of sickness or absenteeism, either suspected or known.
5 Expressed disenchantment or known disagreements about how design and management decisions have been or are being taken.

Once the decision-makers are persuaded that what occurs at present is not wholly satisfactory, you have to then convince them that what you propose will work. In time these same signs, or lack of them, as well as the short- and long-term benefits gained from using the generic evaluation process, will be the check that the new intervention is successful.

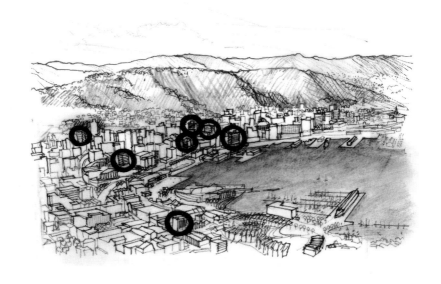

6

Evaluation and facilities management

We have argued in our previous chapters that evaluation is a logical component of designing and managing facilities. In order to make informed decisions for the future, it is logically necessary to take account of the present and review the past. Traditionally building and facilities management concerns have been with portfolio and asset management, and the maintenance and operation of facilities. However, there is growing pressure from building users that such management concerns are not addressing their interests. The serried ranks of clerks have now all but disappeared, to be replaced by a highly qualified, highly mobile workforce that now expects and demands good working conditions and quality surroundings.

> Above all, the success of modern office development depends upon the management of change. Change is everywhere – in equipment, in technology, in what Americans call 'churn', the proportion of the workforce which changes workplace each year (Duffy, 1983).

The rate of churn in US offices has been estimated as high as 60 per cent. Managers are aware that they lack the means to address this phenomenon. However, recognition that there is a need to adopt processes that are responsive to the changing needs of both the individual and the organization is leading some organizations to develop programmes of building evaluation and to offer evaluation services as part of their building resource management responsibilities.

Evaluation programmes are used to accumulate evaluation data, translating it for future use. They are used by building owner and tenant organizations to enhance their corporate knowledge about issues of building ownership and management. They inform their portfolio and asset management activities. In the short-term evaluation programmes have good client-relationship benefits, promoting improved communications, showing a 'caring face'. To promote longer-term benefits, some organizations have set about developing knowledge bases about evaluation outcomes, and through them guidance and advisory material for themselves and their clients. In addition, for some building design and management organizations, the basic market question 'What can we offer clients that others cannot offer?' is being asked. Clearly one answer is to offer evaluation services, which can enhance an organization's responses to problems raised by the changing workforce. Change in the modern workplace is having its profoundest effects on the way people use and operate in buildings. A major concern is how organizations and their managers respond to the challenges of change. Currently, facilities managers lack the tools to address the needs of an organization's most valuable asset – its people. However, some building delivery agencies now offer evaluation activities as part of their client services, providing both the agency and the client with a continuing relationship through a building's development and use.

In this chapter we discuss the development of programmes of building evaluation and the provision of evaluation services. We begin by describing our own experiences with developing a programme of building evaluation with the New Zealand Ministry of Works and Development (MWD). We then make reference to some of the other programmes and evaluation activities of which we have knowledge. We finish by reflecting on the creation of knowledge bases from the information gained through evaluation.

New Zealand Ministry of Works and Development (MWD)

The development of programmes of building evaluation has been led by public-sector and research organizations. Since the early

Figure 6.1 *MWD district offices – locations.*

1980s we have had the support and collaboration of MWD in developing our evaluation process. It is a relatively rare situation for a large government agency to make building evaluation part of its building delivery and management policy. When we began, MWD was a government ministry with an Architectural Division as a building design and management practice under the Government Architect. The Division operated from seven district offices, with its Head Office in Wellington (Figure 6.1). To support its advisory service to central government and government departments, the Division undertook design and supervision of an annual capital works programme that represented about 20 per cent of the total annual expenditure by government on buildings in New Zealand. The work was carried out by the district offices, with a total staff complement of 750 personnel, 150 of whom were architects.

MWD asked us to study user requirements in buildings. It wanted to improve its accountability and ability to give advice to government about its building assets. We suggested the study should be an integral part of a broader investigation of methods for evaluating buildings in use. This developed into a research project whose aim was 'to design, test and implement a practical programme for conducting evaluations of government buildings'. However, we found that the concept of a programme for evaluating buildings in use promulgated by Head Office consistently met with scepticism and resistance in the districts. 'It is difficult enough to do the job we have to do, let alone have to answer all sorts of questions from Head Office and supply them with more data on our projects, which they don't use for any useful purpose anyway'. District offices saw themselves as autonomous practices. While most staff could see benefits from evaluations such as fine-tuning existing buildings, improving the design of future buildings, and establishing high standards, middle management resisted change. There were two main reasons:

1 A new service was perceived as more work. There was neither time nor money to fit in this extra effort. It was a 'good idea' so long as it was 'someone else's job'.
2 Evaluation was perceived as something that would open the way for criticism of individual and collective performance both within MWD and by their clients. It was feared that the clients would be handed a new tool to whip MWD. There was talk of the possibility of being sued by clients. The expectation was that evaluations would be entirely negative, only serving to verify faults.

In addition to this apparent lack of commitment in the districts, we were also advised by Head Office that any proposal must 'take no time and cost nothing'. While this was said partly in jest, it was clear that whatever we proposed must have low cost and time implications.

Initially we had to gain some understanding of the organizational context in which the programme would operate. Bob Shibley, who had experience of developing evaluation programmes for the US Army Corps of Engineers, suggested to us that in any organizational context two basic principles would need to apply if an evaluation programme was to take hold. The evaluation programme operates in a manner characterized by responses to the two principles:

- *Information has to be asked for* – information from evaluation activities will not be used if nobody needs or asks for it.

  Evaluations are non-mandatory; no one has to do them. The programme operates on a 'bottom up' rather than a 'top down' basis. Evaluations are largely generated and conducted from district level. The idea to evaluate emanates from someone with an interest in the building (user, tenant, designer, owner) asking for it. A request can be made to anyone in a district or Head Office. Management's role is to support and nurture the programme, by disseminating information about it, giving assistance to evaluation activities, and providing action on recommendations.
- *People have to be 'vulnerable', willing to change* – people need to be prepared to adjust what they do now to get what they need or ask for.

  Evaluation is integrated with other normal services as much as possible. Evaluation is an inherent part of most architects' mode of operation. In the early stages of the design process it is very common for an architect to seek out buildings of similar type and to evaluate them informally through reading journal articles or where possible making a brief visit or having discussions with colleagues. Tapping in to this normal activity is a key to integrating more formal and rigorous evaluation into the design process. Matching it to current practice increases its appeal to both designers and their clients, and encourages their 'vulnerability'.

To help move from some of the initial scepticism to support, we designed the evaluation programme to allow wide participation by, and negotiation with, all those likely to be affected by its introduction. This occurred through seminars, workshops and interviews with MWD personnel. 'Brush fire' seminars were conducted throughout the country to inform personnel of the division about progress, and to support discussion and negotiation with them about the form the programme should take. The idea of the brush fire was to kindle a flame that would hopefully catch fire and spread information about the evaluation programme throughout MWD and its client departments (Figure 6.2). We gave emphasis to making the evaluation processes and the programme 'fit' with other design and management activities. Later we conducted workshops to prepare facilitators from MWD and its clients to undertake evaluations. We also met senior MWD managers to prepare them for their role of nurturing the programme when it was in place. They declared their commitment to the programme and the actions they would take individually to nurture it.

When the programme was in place and a number of evaluations had been completed, a major audit of the programme was undertaken. Its aim was to determine how well-established the

Figure 6.2 *'Brush fire' seminar. The generic process and typical outcomes are being explained to MWD staff in a district office.*

programme had become and how it could be further developed to respond to the needs of MWD and its clients (Gould *et al.*, 1984). This required over fifty interviews with staff as well as fact finding seminars in each district. The audit found that not everyone was aware of the programme or, more specifically, the outcomes of particular evaluations. However, those who had been directly concerned with evaluations were enthusiastic. They had found them personally informative and rewarding, and wanted to do more. The short-term benefits were seen by them as extremely valuable. The evaluation reports were, however, seen to be of much less value and concern was expressed about the longer-term value of the programme to MWD.

Recent restructuring has converted the Ministry of Works and Development into the state-owned Works and Development Services Corporation (NZ) Ltd (WORKS), which operates as a private-sector corporation. Commercialization means that WORKS must compete for all its work on the open market; government departments are now free to commission any private firm they wish, and WORKS has a number of private clients. In its restructured form WORKS has a central technical support group, which provides co-ordination and technical support to the branch offices. The group is committed to continuing development of evaluation services. Its role is clearly not to control the use of evaluation methods, but to support the evaluation activities of the branch offices and to act as a repository for evaluation outcomes, their recording and analysis.

In addition, the services offered by WORKS have been redefined so that evaluations are an identified structural part of those services. An aim of the central technical support group is to provide and maintain a constituency in the branches for evaluations, and to spell out more clearly the aims and benefits of evaluation by improving the knowledge and marketing of the service they provide for potential clients. The technical support group will also continue to develop its facilitation skills while maintaining the principle that the people with various interests in a building are the ones who evaluate it. Our own research group, now constituted as part of Victoria University's Centre for Building Performance Research, has formed a joint venture with WORKS to help achieve these aims, and to continue to explore applications and develop adaptations of the process that may make it easier for those engaged in the work to achieve their desired aims. It is clear, from WORKS' point of view, that there is a need for a supply marketing strategy for evaluations that aims to sell the existing product, as well as a demand strategy that will benefit most from new adaptations and from information about their application. Experience suggests that both strategies are most effective when used in concert.

Other evaluation programmes

A number of other programmes of evaluation have grown out of developments in what is known as Post Occupancy Evaluation (POE). POE simply means the evaluation of a building after it has been occupied. A number of organizations in both the private and public sector, particularly in the US, offer POE services. POE is now a discipline of its own. According to Preiser *et al.* (1988), POE is a phase in the building process that follows the sequence of planning, programming, design, construction and occupancy of a building. In this model its emphasis is clearly retrospective – comparison with previously stated norms preferably from the original design brief or programme, rather than pro-active. POE is seen as informing regulation and guidance documentation rather than offering methods or direct advice to designers and managers on how they should access and use knowledge about people and buildings. Through POE there is developing a growing knowledge base about the relationships of people and buildings. However, there remains a concern that the major issue of providing information that is directly usable by building designers, managers and users is not being addressed. POE information often remains as reports and documents, inaccessible to those who can most benefit from their findings.

The seminal work in this field is that of the Building Performance Research Unit (BPRU) at the University of Strathclyde in the late 1960s. Their book, *Building Performance* (BPRU, 1972), described the the work of a research unit comprising an architect, an operational research scientist, a psychologist, a quantity surveyor, a systems analyst and a physicist. They developed a series of techniques for the appraisal of over fifty comprehensive schools in Scotland. For possibly the first time the techniques related space and its organization to people's responses, costs, space use, services and movement. In the 1970s there was increasing development of evaluation and appraisal techniques. Newman's research on crime in high-rise public housing (Newman, 1973) changed housing policy in terms of design in the US. The work of Cooper (1970, 1975), Becker (1974), Francescato *et al.* (1979), Rabinowitz (1975), Marans and Spreckelmeyer (1981), and Preiser (1983) all influenced development in the US. In France, Boudon reported on user response to Le Corbusier's housing at Pessac (1972). In the UK the evaluation work of the Department of Health and Social Security (DHSS) and the Scottish Home and Health Department (SHHD) has made important contributions, as has the Building Research Establishment with its building appraisal studies. The *Architects' Journal* in the UK is one of the few architectural magazines to treat architectural criticism in a non-advocatory way.

Government organizations and corporate bodies have always taken a close interest in POE. Shibley (1985) has suggested that much early evaluation work was characterized by 'the arrogant assumption that outside evaluators somehow knew best what to evaluate, how to evaluate it, how to package the results, and how the "institution" they were serving should proceed as a result of the research'. Nevertheless much influential work has been carried out, particularly by the US Army Corps of Engineers. In 1980 the US government passed legislation requiring government buildings to be evaluated to ensure 'the effectiveness of built and planned public buildings. . . and provision of architecturally distinguished accommodation'.

Kantrowitz, in a review of building evaluation activities (1985), records that, in the US, states such as New Mexico, New York, California and Florida are actively supporting applied work in programming and evaluation. The General Services Administration has adopted a research-based programming process as part of its design-procurement procedures. Federal agencies such as the US Department of Energy, the Department of Housing and Urban Development, the Department of Health Education and Welfare and the US Navy have sponsored work. The work of Farbstein and Kantrowitz (1991) for the US Postal Service is participatory. While employing questionnaire techniques, they adopt a multi-method approach for touring interviews and review activities. While few commit themselves as fully to a participatory approach as WORKS NZ, many are incorporating an increasingly significant element of participatory evaluation in their work. For instance, the programmes operated by Public Works Canada; Health and Welfare Canada; the California Department of Corrections; and the Department of Housing and Construction, Australia, all use participatory methods to some extent.

Bycroft *et al.* (1987) record that Australian developments have drawn heavily on the New Zealand experience, although more recent developments in the Commonwealth Department of Housing and Construction (DHC) are derived from Europe, specifically from the issues raised in the draft International Standard on Building Performance. In describing the work of DHC on evaluation they indicate that a number of Australian government organizations are engaged in evaluation programmes, and cite guidelines published by two major committees responsible for co-ordinating government initiatives in the building industry – the National Committee on Rationalised Building (NCRB) and the National Public Works Conference. According to Bycroft *et al.*, the objectives of the DHC evaluation programme are:

1 To measure departmental performance in terms of:

    (a) quality of product (asset),
    (b) service to client.

2 To appraise facilities in use.
3 To assess the success or otherwise of facilities provided by DHC.

Evaluations are carried out within each state by project teams that are trained in evaluation techniques by central office staff. The main objectives of individual evaluations are to measure the quality of a facility in terms of:

- *Client/user satisfaction:* based primarily on a comprehensive survey of a facility's users and occupants. User satisfaction is measured with a standard survey form referred to as the 'Satisfaction Scale' (Vischer, 1989). The survey also includes the collection of information about the facility's systems, finishes and internal functioning.
- *Fitness for purpose:* based on the client's requirements and the extent to which the facility suits the need or function for which it was provided. The assessment of fitness for purpose includes interviews with a client representative and representatives of

different user groups. In addition, a single-page survey form, referred to as the '+3−3 survey', asks a large number of users to list the three best and three worst aspects of the facility.

- *Technical performance:* an evaluation of the physical performance of the facility by technical experts to measure the performance of building systems such as air-conditioning, acoustics and lighting.
- *Value for cost:* an evaluation of the cost of the facility, including the operational and maintenance costs. Where possible and where information is available, these costs are compared with costs of similar public- and private-sector facilities.

In DHC the findings from evaluations are categorized as action or information findings. The former require immediate corrective or further investigative action. The latter are sorted into further categories based on the main functional groups in the facility delivery process, for the purpose of feeding forward information on buildings to designers, constructors and occupants.

Activities in the private sector have been led in the office field by several furniture companies, which now offer some version of evaluation services to their customers. Herman Miller's activities in this area led to the company's involvement with the foundation of the International Facilities Management Association (IFMA). Zimring and Wener (1985) cite a number of examples of evaluation work in the private sector including Anthony and Bernstein's work with Kaplan McLaughline Diaz, Olsen and Pershing at the Bellevue Hospital Center in New York and Picasso for AT&T. Preiser *et al.* (1988) refer to the work of the Marriott hotel chain in developing prototype hotel units. The work of Duffy in the UK (1983) and Davis *et al.* in the US (1985) in the development of the ORBIT study and other related work demonstrates how evaluation activity can provide design guidance for office development in both the private and public sectors.

While not all the above are examples of institutionalized evaluation programmes, they are evidence of evaluation becoming more and more part of the activities of organizations with responsibilities for a portfolio of buildings. Many use non-participatory approaches, though that too is changing. We have also found that building delivery agencies tend to be slow to follow the trend. As WORKS discovered in its own organization, architects appear to be fixated on the static model of the design process – that their business is the production of new buildings – and are either unable or unwilling to shift to the idea of providing a continuing service to clients. However, in New Zealand a typical comment from client organizations is 'Why haven't we done this before?' One tenant organization told WORKS, 'This is so useful; if you don't use evaluations, we will.'

Knowledge bases

The reasons for an organization developing programmes of evaluation or offering evaluation services often differ from the reasons for conducting a one-off evaluation. Evaluation programmes and services are geared to longer-term benefits, while one-offs promote both immediate and long-term action. Development of evaluation services usually attracts fees and income, while programmes improve an organization's corporate knowledge about buildings it is occupying or dealing with. The long-term value to an organization of an evaluation programme may be considerably enhanced by an operational database, which can be used to influence building acquisition, operational policy and portfolio management. However, it is our experience that the development of a knowledge database is not a straightforward matter.

Organizations contemplating development of a database must consider not only its form and content but also its management. Issues of information transfer are highly problematic. Structuring information and making it accessible to different users is a specialist skill. Maintaining and upgrading the information is a different but equally specialist skill. Reviews of some of the evaluation reports we have produced have shown that the way information is recorded and presented is important to its usefulness in future situations. For example, the knowledge that the users of a particular building did not like the quality of the floor covering is of limited value. What may be needed is why they did not like the quality of the floor covering, the uses to which it is normally put, the reason it was specified in the first place, and some technical details about its specification, performance and maintenance. Ensuring that this quality and depth of information are collected consistently during evaluation processes requires specialist skills for accumulating and translating that information into a form for future use.

With our assistance WORKS has made significant progress in demonstrating the short-term benefits of evaluation. It has only more recently started to consider longer-term benefits, which will come to the organization from development of a database from evaluations. Establishing a database is a specialist activity requiring dedicated people with appropriate skills. It is also one that requires a pro-active approach to evaluations, and this does not sit comfortably with the two principles of 'bottom up' generation and vulnerability, which have guided the WORKS evaluation programme so far. It is also difficult to justify within the now fully commercial operation of WORKS. In order to acquire the necessary data, evaluation specialists may have to initiate evaluations based on their own interests, and specify particular methods of data collection that are not necessarily in the immediate interests of the owner or users of the building concerned.

The question now facing WORKS is who will pay for assembling information that is not of immediate interest to its clients, and which is therefore not of immediate commercial value. This kind of activity would be consistent with the mandate of a government department, such as the former Ministry of Works and Development, charged with responsibility for ensuring quality in government building programmes. But WORKS has no such mandate, and can only undertake tasks of short-term interest for which clients will pay. It seems likely that for WORKS the long-term interests will have to be addressed in commercial terms, and will depend upon projections of the growth and profitability of the evaluation business. The long-term interests would also be served if a major client could be persuaded to fund the development of a database to benefit its own building programme – as do Health and Welfare Canada and the California Department of Corrections. The very different demands that short- and long-term interests make on the evaluation effort have yet to be successfully integrated in fully commercial design and construction enterprises.

The use to which a database may be put can take many forms. The US Army Corps of Engineers' very thorough Design Guide Publication series offers one model, as does similar guidance documentation produced by the DHSS and SHHD in the UK. The production, publication and dissemination of a guidance series is a major undertaking for any organization, and is difficult to keep up to date without a significant commitment of resources. Another model is to integrate evaluation data into a computerized information system similar to that developed by the Australian Department of Housing and Construction. Its system, called POETIC, uses a customized form of standard database software for the analysis, sorting, storage and retrieval of information generated by evaluation. Reports from evaluations conducted by means of our generic process have been used to categorize evaluation outcomes to reflect the concerns of the following interest groups:

1 Policy and brief (owner, client).
2 Design and construction (designers, builders).
3 Operation and maintenance (occupants, managers, maintenance staff).
4 Fine-tuning (all groups).

The information provided in this way was also cross-referenced to a general building documentation and classification system to provide a further means for disseminating information from evaluations. We have, however, found generally that on-line databases are difficult to maintain and are not well used in design or management practice.

We are therefore wary of giving too much priority to the development of knowledge databases. For us, action is the prime purpose of and motivation for the evaluation activities we have described. Nevertheless we believe that action should include recording and reporting what occurred at each evaluation event. While such reports are useful of themselves in promoting action, the reports collectively form part of our corporate knowledge about people, organizations and buildings. We have not used such reports for significant database analysis or interpretation, nor to move towards the development of guideline documentation for specific building types or situations. Effective analysis and interpretation may in time provide such long-term organizational and general knowledge benefits. However, our principal use of the data gathered from evaluation has been to assist development of what we have called a checklist of factors.

The checklist is a framework that begins to describe the relationship of people, organizations and buildings. We have set out the checklist under six major attribute headings: Corporate,

Table 6.1   Comparison of ICF and CBPR categories for comparative evaluation of office buildings.

International Centre for Facilities Ottawa, Ontario, Canada	Centre for Building Performance Research, Wellington, New Zealand
Location, access and wayfinding	Access and circulation
Support for office work	
Meetings and group work	
Change and churn by occupants	
Physical protection	
Amenities	Amenities
Image to public and occupants	Presentation
Special facilities	
Work outside normal hours and conditions	Business services
Office information technology	
Sound and visual environment	
Thermal environment and indoor air	Working environment
Manageability	
Cleanliness	Building manageability
Structure and building envelope	Structural considerations
Layout and building factors	Space functionality
	Health and safety

Site, Construction, Space, Internal environment, and Building services.

The Centre for Building Performance Research in Wellington has used these attribute headings to develop a system of weighted scales for scoring the quality of office buildings. This system, now being marketed by a private sector client as 'Building Quality Assessment' (BQA), enables property owners to measure and compare the quality of buildings for investment purposes (Beddek and Kernohan, 1990). In Canada, the International Centre for Facilities (ICF) in Ottawa has pioneered development of 'Serviceability Scales' for use by Public Works Canada (PWC) to rate the quality of office facilities used by Canadian government departments. The Serviceability Scales are also used to assist departments to specify their generic requirements for office accommodation

(Davis et al., in press). A version of the PWC Serviceability Scales is in the process of ballot for publication by the American Society for Testing and Materials (ASTM).

The serviceability concept differs from the BQA performance concept because the former focuses on occupant concerns with facilities, whereas the latter addresses investor concerns. However, the two instruments are analogous in the way they employ sets of descriptors for different levels of performance, covering many features of a building. Table 6.1 shows the principal categories adopted by ICF and CBPR for comparative evaluation of the quality of office buildings. It is our view that such checklist-based evaluation systems, devised by experts but informed by experience with participatory evaluation processes, have an important function in providing a means of comparing different buildings on a common basis. Such comparison is very important to organizations wishing to choose between many optional buildings, and for companies and institutions that manage a large portfolio of facilities. Comprehensive systems such as Serviceability and BQA are costly and time-consuming to develop, but become, in time, reliable and efficient instruments.

A checklist should never be used as the sole means of evaluating a building at the exploratory level. Used as part of participatory evaluations, it can aid comprehensive evaluation by complementing participatory activities and helping to ensure that recommendations for action are stated as part of an understanding of the wider building context. Checklists can provide a structure and format for a consistent recording of the outcomes of evaluations, a basic requirement of any knowledge database and for its management.

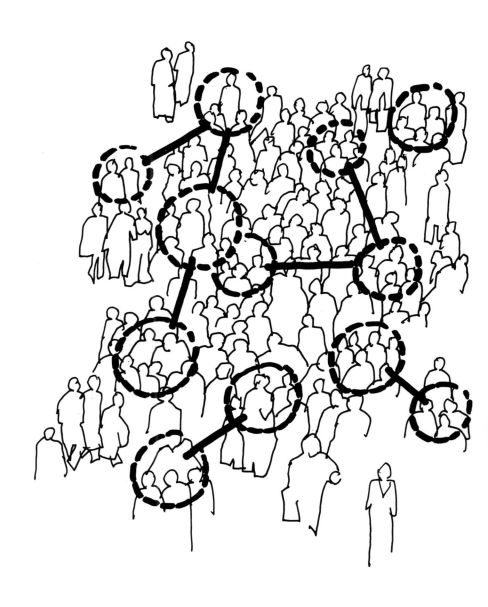

7

Gaining experiential knowledge through dialogue

Our research work began from a pragmatic rather than a theoretical base. We were asked, as architects, to find out how information about building user requirements could improve the design and management of buildings. We had it in our minds to develop a tool to record people's perceptions about what works well and what not so well in buildings. We assumed that with such knowledge of people's perceptions we could state some universal truths about the relations of people and buildings. From these universal truths prescriptive advice could then be given to designers and managers, to the benefit of all. The generic evaluation process was first developed and used on this somewhat ambitious and naive premise.

Using the process, we learned that:

1 The knowledge of users and providers is significantly different.
2 Building-users hold a wealth of experiential knowledge of buildings that is not being used to inform design and management processes.
3 Much information is specific to the particular building evaluated.
4 Prescriptive advice is difficult to produce and is unlikely to address the changing circumstances and values of users and providers effectively.

We have concluded that for the design and management of facilities to be responsive to the changing needs of users and providers, there is a need to integrate the knowledge both hold, and that such integration only occurs through dialogue.

Using the generic evaluation process taught us about the nature of knowledge and the importance of dialogue. We found that the dialogue between users and providers set up by the process was a rich learning experience for all. Those who have experienced the process have acknowledged this, and expressed surprise that such dialogue does not happen as a matter of routine. Our work progressed from the realization that here, in the process, was a source of knowledge about the design and management of facilities. In this final chapter we discuss some of the things we have learned about the nature of user and provider knowledge, and explain how we think experiential knowledge, fostered by the generic evaluation process, contributes to new ways of knowing through dialogue.

The nature of user knowledge

Users know about buildings through experiencing them. Their knowledge is gained in the course of living and working in buildings through their day to day interactions of people and the built environment. People respond to buildings in physical, emotional and intellectual ways. Many responses are subconscious. We enter a room. It is too warm or too cold, too bright, the air smells fresh, the colour scheme is cheerful. We may not note all these things explicitly but they register. When we are familiar with a place, our thoughts are more particular. I need another light, a better chair. We need more power points. Why can't I control the temperature? Wayne Attoe (1978) suggests that every response people make to the environment is a form of criticism or evaluation. It is this knowledge we need to 'tap into'.

User knowledge is experiential knowledge, which is a special way of knowing and thinking. It is knowledge that is concerned with the immediate realities of one's situation, not with abstract theories about it. It is integrated with the rest of life. At an individual level it relates to a person's needs to learn and develop. Fritz Steele (1973) identifies six categories to describe the nature of people's experience of the physical environment. We find these to be consistent with what it is that users expect of buildings:

- *Security and shelter* – refers to protection from unwanted stimuli in one's surroundings.
- *Social contact* – refers to the arrangements of facilities and spaces that permit or promote social interaction.
- *Symbolic identification* – refers to the messages sent by settings that tell someone what a person, group, or organization is like.
- *Task instrumentality* – refers to the facilities and layouts appropriate for carrying out tasks in a particular setting.
- *Pleasure* – refers to the pleasure or gratification a place gives to those who use it.
- *Growth* – refers to the stimulus for growth the setting gives the user.

Users' experience and understanding of buildings are important, because they have direct meaning for them and affect the way they use a building. It is informal knowledge, not easily accessed and generally not recorded. It is variable. The same place can have different meanings at different times and in different social situations. There is a small retreat chapel near where we work. We take architecture students there because we think it is one of New Zealand's finest buildings. If we go there on a sunny day, we do not have to convince them. The light through the coloured glass falls on the granite altar in a remarkable fashion. It is a true architectural experience. On a dull day you notice the stains on the roughcast under the windows and the ugly heaters on the wall. The students are disillusioned. We have to assure them it is good architecture. Some believe us because we are their tutors. Others remain unconvinced. Their definitions of design quality are influenced by changing physical and social circumstances. Ellis and Joiner (1985) state: 'Social experience is continuously accumulating and changing, and so meaning in environment is negotiable and temporary. Design and operational quality is therefore negotiable'.

When we 'tap' user knowledge, it provides an abundant source of information about buildings. But providers perceive user knowledge as largely subjective. To them, it exists in forms that are not systematic, not ordered, not necessarily rational, not consistent over time. Such knowledge is a 'matter of opinion', imprecise, transitory and uncertain. 'People change their minds.' How can one design for that? How can one manage people's idiosyncrasies? It is impossible to meet everyone's needs.

The nature of provider knowledge

Provider knowledge is gained initially through education and training. It is largely received knowledge. For example, we (the authors) are architects. We learned about architecture at universities in different parts of the world but within a common Western academic tradition. In lectures we learned the body of the accepted knowledge of the discipline – the traditions and procedures of architecture as history, and the principles of professionalism that have been its underpinnings since the mid-1800s. In studio we learned by doing design projects and through criticism of what we were doing – criticism by ourselves, our peers and tutors. Most of the discussion was philosophical, aesthetic and technical in nature, about the physical artifact, its significance and how to produce it. Hardly any time was devoted to the operation and use of the artifact. In due course we 'topped up' up these academic foundations through professional experience – from client meetings, designing, producing, and constructing buildings and seeing what our architect colleagues elsewhere were up to. To some extent this added to and superseded the body of received knowledge, but without the systematic or discursive learning of our earlier academic studies.

Building design and management professionals take a pragmatic view to acquiring the knowledge they need to practise. They think rules, regulations and codes are ideal; they spell out what can and cannot be done. Bits of prescriptive advice (rules of thumb) help. User requirements must be described as norms and averages – 'the average person'. User participation means consultation with the client and a few senior managers. Mackinder and Marvin in their study of design decision-making in architectural practice in the UK (1982) showed that:

> Designers based their decisions largely on personal and practice experience and that they used few publications . . . any information that designers consult must be quick and easy to absorb . . . (in the early stages of design) they used the few publications they did consult mainly to check or develop concepts they had already formed . . . (from the detailed design stage onward) designers had to consult more publications; but the level of use was often still low . . . manufacturers were the

main source consulted; they were preferred to official publications . . . designers tend to know and use a repeatedly small, random personal selection of the technical information available . . . the research gave a strong indication that designers tend to seek written information as a last resort.

Trade literature and professional magazines are what architects read. They read the magazines to see what their peers are doing, what is being built and what it looks like. In some respects reading an architectural magazine is for architects a continuation of the peer and tutor criticisms they were familiar with as students, though much less threatening. The magazines have great influence on the profession, yet they focus mostly on the philosophical and aesthetic concerns of architecture. They address only part of the knowledge needed by architects.

Architectural and building research extend beyond philosophy and aesthetics. Building performance and environment behaviour research in particular hold abundant technical information – some would say too much. Architects and other design and management professionals are assailed on all sides by information – new construction methods, materials, products, technologies; new regulations, codes, standards, guidelines. Most countries operate building research establishments, and their publications are a well-respected part of the vast body of knowledge available. Building performance encompasses measurable phenomena in areas of health and safety, energy, building failure, and management techniques, among others. It is generally concerned with buildings as artefacts. Methods of measurement are well tried and tested in all these areas.

Environment behaviour research is closely aligned with the concerns of users. It is largely descriptive, explaining what people do in buildings, what is there and how it is used. It has been defined as 'the study of the mutual relations between human beings and the physical environment at all scales, and applications of the knowledge thus gained to improving the quality of life through better informed environmental policy, planning, design and education' (Zube and Moore, 1987). As such, the field includes environmental perception and cognition, socio-behavioural research, facility programming, environmental evaluation and research utilization. Much activity is concerned with researching environment-behaviour relationships in the classic scientific mode with a view to discovering laws and forming theories that may provide rules for providers to follow. In spite of this, no satisfactory theories have as yet been expounded:

> There is a binding assumption that somewhere out there, there are fixed and immutable laws linking environment and behaviour to be found. The possibility that the quest may be illusory and that there are actually rather few generalities of any significance about environmental behaviour to be found has not taken hold (Ellis, 1983).

Research, particularly environment behaviour research, has often been advocated as the means for linking user and provider knowledge. However, the acknowledged gap between academic theory and practice suggests that many people are unconvinced that research can form appropriate links between users and providers. Prescriptive advice about people's behaviour is difficult to produce. This lack makes much of the information the field may have to offer unsuitable to providers and their current modes of receiving knowledge.

Linking user and provider knowledge

Traditionally researchers, when providing knowledge for designers, have operated from a Newtonian model that is static, deterministic and objective. Schon's 'hard, dry ground . . . of well formed problems' (1983) is the territory of this traditional approach, which is characterized by the separation of user, provider and researcher. Schneekloth (1987) illustrates the results of researchers and providers operating remotely:

> Information transfer. . . is based on the understanding that knowledge is generated in one sphere, sent out into the world, and picked up and used by others who are potential consumers of research results. This form assumes a non-interventionist stance. It uses scientific conventions on the one hand, and the application of knowledge on the other. The relationship between the generation of knowledge and its subsequent use is discontinuous and the time frame indeterminant.

Similar relationships exist between provider and user. Farbstein and Kantrowitz (1991) have used the metaphor of the swampy terrain below the hard, dry ground of the researcher and provider to describe the world of the user. It is where 'pressure for answers is constant and professional boundaries are often unclear'. The world of the user is where change and uncertainty prevail. Such a world threatens research and provider knowledge because no 'average person' lives there. Information cannot be easily abstracted or generalized. This threatens to undermine the power of researchers and providers, who, otherwise, on the hard dry ground, currently have control of the totality of knowledge in building.

At present, for most providers, it is possible to construct without user knowledge. Many would argue that such a strategy is less bothersome and less expensive. The idea that they might begin to shift their cultural alignments and consciously learn about user knowledge would seem pointless. Yet for some providers, who have begun to shift their alignments and take up with processes such as ours, the benefits of experiential learning have proved significant. The principal rewards have occurred through the dialogue created. Architects from WORKS, some of whom have been participants or facilitators in the evaluation process, agree that for them the greatest benefit of using the generic evaluation process was not so much the information gathered but the experience of learning from the views and insights of others. They had never before taken the opportunity to collaborate with the people their work affected. There had never seemed to be the need. For some the richness of the experience was a revelation. Providers can of course continue to ignore user knowledge if they choose, but it is no way to design and manage better buildings – and users know it.

Our approach to participatory building evaluation is to explore a way of knowing that is different to what we see as the traditional scientific way in which providers and researchers obtain or receive knowledge. To address the specific day to day needs of users and providers in a changing world, we need to form temporary alliances of users, providers and perhaps researchers too, to benefit all three. We have come to this view through the experience of using the generic evaluation process.

'What we are able to know is grounded in the way we organize to know' (Schneekloth and Shibley, 1990). What we are proposing is that through experiential learning and dialogue we can begin a cultural transformation in which all participants, users and providers, bring their expertise to bear, have an equal 'say'. They all have the opportunity to express their understandings from their own culture, while respecting the values of the others.

Historically, the beginnings of what we advocate lie in action research and user participation. Wisner *et al.* (1991) compare Lewin's view of action research with the intellectual movements of the 1920s, 1930s and 1940s in Latin America and Asia. They discuss participation as action or praxis, which stresses the process of participation itself rather than the physical outcomes. They distinguish between 'instrumental' and 'transformative' participation. The former is concerned with efficiency and effectiveness, while the latter 'is seen to facilitate changing social consciousness. . .' They note that participation itself need not necessarily imply a democratic process, and refer to Foucault's belief (1980) that the inseparability of power and knowledge precludes all possibility of 'neutral' relations between research/designers and client/participants. They question the possibility of co-equal participation of citizen and researcher alike.

Farbstein and Kantrowitz (1991) introduce the term 'design–decision research'. They suggest it is part of a new paradigm that addresses the context of design. It is part of a continuum that allows design and research to be performed simultaneously – a different way of thinking and acting in relation to the design process. 'It focuses explicitly on helping clients realize their objectives. . . The researcher's role is to help the organization make its own best decisions within the context of its objectives'.

The outcomes of design–decision research affect decision-making directly. Farbstein and Kantrowitz recognize that the client's identity and character affect how such research can be carried out. Similar thinking pervades the work of Schneekloth and Shibley (1990), who use the term 'dialogic practice' to define what they do in their design and management activities. They proceed on a basis that includes clients and building users as co-researchers as both the consultant and the client work to make some sense of organizational problems. They assume 'that knowledge is socially constructed through dialogue within relationships. That knowledge is not an abstraction "out there" but is generated and confirmed within networks of relationships in a dialectic between concrete knowing and abstract knowing.'

In justifying that view, they refer to Belenky *et al.*'s 'The Collaborative' (1986), which identifies five perspectives on knowing. These illustrate that clearly there are other ways of knowing than the rational and technical. They include silence, received knowledge, subjective knowledge, procedural knowledge, and constructed knowledge. The findings of Belenky *et al.* draw on interviews as well as literature on cognitive development and moral reasoning. They note:

> The women tended to focus on listening to acquire knowledge and procedures, to define themselves in relation to others and their ideas. The men were more inclined to lecture from authority, to define themselves as separate from others. . . These differences are further revealed in the masculine form of subjective knowing which leads to the statement 'I have a right to be heard' in contrast with the feminine statement 'it is only my opinion'. . . those differences are in the intention to differentiate versus the intention to be in relationship. . . the purpose of knowing for men was justification, while for women it was understanding and connection.

Our approach is 'transformative' and has much in common with design–decision research and dialogic practice. What we are advocating is a temporary alliance of users, providers and researchers to benefit from each other's knowledge through dialogue. We are not suggesting that dialogue is without conflict, but it is the commitment to dialogue that offers the possibility of developing awareness and new forms of knowledge. We believe our process of participatory evaluation, of dialogue, of negotiation, is a lever that can contribute to the design and operation of better places for people. In our final comments we outline the dimensions of effective dialogue and how they have been applied in using our evaluation process.

Integrating knowledge through dialogue

Paulo Freire (1973) has argued that successful dialogue has two essential dimensions, those of reflection and action. From our experience we think it useful to add two more dimensions that are particularly relevant to the evaluation of facilities. The first of these is collaboration, through which people agree to work together in a temporary alliance. The second is negotiation, by which people transform their reflections on the facility into practical recommendations for action. It is the combined presence of these four dimensions that characterize successful dialogue for evaluating facilities.

Dialogue leading to collaboration

Every project for provision or change in a facility requires the bringing together of people. A temporary alliance is formed so that those chosen can work together on the project. Those who participate do so because it is perceived they are able to bring to the project some expertise or knowledge that is necessary for its success. We have shown that the expertise or knowledge that people acquire is gained in a cultural framework with shared values and ways of working. The knowledge of users comes from experiencing facilities directly, and is rarely institutionalized as part of the culture of the organization. The knowledge of providers tends to be taught formally, and is institutionalized within professional organizations. Traditionally the knowledge of providers is privileged over the knowledge of users, because providers believe in what they do and users accept their expertise. In Chapter 2 we outlined five stages of cross-cultural awareness. It is salutary to see that only at stage three do people become consciously aware of cultural differences, and at stage four become committed to working towards a better understanding among different groups. Thus it takes considerable awareness, and such qualities as openness and empathy, before people are willing to risk their values and knowledge with others they perceive as different. It is not surprising therefore that providers rarely initiate collaboration with users, and that users largely remain unaware of ways to communicate with providers. We find that engaging in dialogue centred around the activity of facility evaluation contributes to a new form of temporary alliance, where more equitable collaboration between users and providers occurs. This collaboration not only brings to the temporary alliance the expertise of those involved, it also requires 'a willingness to be vulnerable to each other's ways of knowing' (Schneekloth and Shibley, 1990).

Dialogue requires reflection

Users asked to evaluate facilities have no difficulty in articulating and expressing their views. This critical capacity and even enthusiasm of users not only to notice their surroundings, but also make some assessment of how well the facility works or does not work, is intensified when people with similar interests agree to exchange views. Because they are focusing on parts of the facility that hold interest to them, they are able not only to identify those parts that work or do not work, but also explore the reasons why they perceive it that way. The key ingredient in this process is the facility itself. It is the concrete reality that all providers and users share in common. Perceptive reflection occurs by directly encountering the facility. The facility mediates the sharing of a common experience, thereby assisting those present to encounter each other's perceptions and values. This sharing is the basis for successful negotiation and debate, providing a way in which users and providers can come to 'know' together. We have suggested in this book that a way of doing this is consciously and systematically to walk through the facility. Even if the facility under investigation is not yet constructed, there will be drawings or a model that represent the design. In this case the drawings or model can be 'walked through' in a way that is analogous to a touring interview of a constructed facility. Through this process of reflection, each person is able to articulate his/her particular view of the facility.

Dialogue promotes negotiation

We have termed the dialogue set up by our evaluation process social negotiation. We see it primarily as an informally occurring dialogue, growing out of an increasing level of awareness and understanding for the point of view of others. It comprises face-to-face discussions and negotiation. The evaluation process creates social situations in which people feel free and have equal opportunity to engage in negotiation through dialogue, and while differences are acknowledged, no one group's view is privileged. The primacy of rational and technical knowledge can no longer be assumed. Equal credence has to be given to values, intentions, perceptions. The way people come to know takes on significance. People may resist knowledge imposed or hierarchically created, but develop a commitment to knowledge that emerges through dialogue. If people have come together in a temporary alliance then it seems appropriate that a unity of purpose is negotiated for each project. The right to define quality does not reside with one group more than another.

Dialogue demands action

Even when the other three dimensions of dialogue are successfully in place, there is no guarantee that action will follow. It must be remembered that the alliance is only temporary. Once the alliance is disbanded, those taking part tend to return to the ways and values of their culture. Thus users attend to the pressures of their normal job and providers turn their attention to the next project. Yet ensuring that action is taken to implement what has been negotiated is critical to the success of the intervention. We have shown that there are multiple benefits from using the generic evaluation process, physical and social, both immediate and long-term. Often the changes recommended are organizational, a result of at last talking about an issue and sorting it out face to face. If there is no resulting action, then the facility remains unchanged. No transformation has occurred and the purpose of the intervention remains unrealized. Those who have taken part still learn something from the collaboration, but such learning is likely to be tainted with a lack of trust, resulting in the avoidance of such collaboration in the future. Once the evaluation event is over, everyone needs to know what happened. What are the outcomes and what is to happen now? Dialogue must continue in some form. To maintain the goodwill generated, communication needs to be as much as possible face to face, through meetings and seminars.

Postcript

Where issues about designing and managing building facilities are concerned, providers' interests currently dominate or are privileged over those of users. The result is facilities skewed to the providers' view of the world, a world in which users needs are absent, or at least relegated in importance. Our response has been to develop a generic evaluation process to transform this situation so that user experience, knowledge and values gain a rightful place. Both users and providers depend on each other. Users and providers have a right to their own culture. We are not replacing anyone's job. However, to produce better facilities, particularly for users, there is a need to develop more cross-cultural awareness. The key to integrating user and provider knowledge is sharing knowledge through social negotiation. We have described what we believe are the essential dimensions of such dialogue, but dialogue by itself will not transform anything until users, and providers in particular, acknowledge their interdependence and need for better understanding. Participatory building evaluation based on the generic evaluation process described in this book is a 'lever to move the rock'.

Bibliography

Allen, T. H. (1978) *New Methods in Social Science*, pp. 119–31 (New York: Praeger).

Attoe, Wayne (1978) *Architecture and Critical Imagination* (New York: John Wiley and Sons).

Becker, Franklin D. (1974) *Design for Living – the Resident's view of Multi-Family Housing* (Ithaca, New York: Center for Urban Development Research, Cornell University).

Becker, Franklin (1990) *The Total Workplace – Facilities Management and the Elastic Organization* (New York: Van Nostrand Reinhold).

Beddek, Peter and Kernohan, David (1990) 'Measurement of Quality in Buildings', in *Building for the 90s: Proceedings of the Biennial Conference of the New Zealand Institute of Building*, edited by Richard Aynsley, pp. 29–36 (Auckland: NZIOB).

Belenky, M. F., Clinchy, B. M., Goldberger, N. R. and Tarule, J. M. (1986) 'The Collaborative', in *Women's Ways of Knowing: The Development of Self, Voice, and Mind* (New York: Basic Books).

Boudon, Philippe (1972) *Lived in Architecture*, 1st English Edition (London: Lund Humphries).

Building Performance Research Unit (1972) *Building Performance* (London: Applied Science Publishers).

Bycroft Peter, Thompson, Judy and Bateman, Gail (1987) *Post Occupancy Evaluation in an Australian Context* (Canberra: Department of Housing and Construction).

Cooper, Clare (1970) *Resident's Attitudes towards the Environment at St Francis Square, San Francisco* (Berkeley: University of California, Institute of Urban and Regional Development).

Cooper, Clare (1975) *Easter Hill Village: Some Social Aspects of Design* (New York: The Free Press).

Davis, G. (1982) 'The Relationship of Evaluation to Facilities Programming,' paper presented at a symposium on evaluation of occupied designed environments (Georgia Institute of Technology).

Davis, G., Becker, F. Duffy, F. and Sims, W. (1985) *ORBIT-2: Organizations, Buildings and Information Technology* (Norwalk, Conn.: Harbinger).

Davis, G., Gray J. and Sinclair D. (forthcoming) *Buildings that Work* (Ottawa: International Centre for Facilities).

Duffy, Frank (1983) *The Orbit Study: Information Technology and Office Design* (London: DEGW and EOSYS Ltd).

Ellis, Peter (1983) 'Institutional Problems with Design Research in Britain'. In *Proceedings of the Conference on People and Physical Environment Research* (Wellington, 1983), edited by Duncan Joiner, Geoffrey Brimilcombe, John Daish, John Gray and David Kernohan, pp. 428–37 (Wellington: NZ Ministry of Works and Development).

Ellis , Peter and Joiner, Duncan (1985) 'Design Quality is negotiable', in *Place and Placemaking: Proceedings of the Conference on People and Physical Environment Research* (Melbourne, 1985), edited by Kim Dovey, Peter Downton and Greg Missingham, pp. 123–35 (Melbourne: PAPER).

Farbstein, Jay and Kantrowitz, Min (1991) 'Design Research in the Swamp – Towards a New Paradigm', in *Advances in Environment, Behavior, and Design*, Vol. 3, edited by Ervin H. Zube and Gary T. Moore, pp. 297–318 (New York: Plenum Press).

Francescato, G., et al. (1979) *Resident's Satisfaction in HUD-assisted Housing: Design and Management Factors* (Washington DC: US Department of Housing and Urban Development, US Government Printing Office).

Foucault, M. (1980) *Power/Knowledge* (C. Gordon, ed.) (New York: Beacon).

Freire, P. (1973) *Pedagogy of the Oppressed* (New York: Seabury).

Gould, K., with Daish, J. Gray, J. and Kernohan, D. (1984) *Audit of the MWD Programme of post occupancy evaluation: 1980–1983* (Wellington, New Zealand: School of Architecture Publications, Victoria University of Wellington).

Holmes, Anna (1989) *Womanhood: a new vision of women's health and wellbeing* (Collins Dove, Blackburn, Victoria).

Kantrowitz, Min (1985) 'Has Environment Behavior Research made a difference?' *Environment and Behavior*, 17:1, pp. 25–46 (New York: Sage).

Laing, Patricia (1988) 'Friendly pain: personal growth and bicultural development', paper prepared for a series of bicultural workshops for health managers in Wellington, New Zealand.

Le Compte, William F. (1974) 'Behaviour settings as Data-generating Units for the Environmental Planner and Architect', in *Designing for Human Behavior: Architecture and the Behavioral Sciences*, edited by J. Lang et al., pp. 183–93 (Stroudsburg, PA. : Dowden, Hutchinson and Ross).

Lewin, K. (1946) 'Action Research and minority problems', *Journal of Social Issues*, 1–2, pp. 34–6.

Mackinder, M. and Marvin, H. (1982) *Design Decision Making in Architectural Practice*, BRE Information Paper IP 11/82 (Garston, UK: Building Research Station).

Marans, R. and K. Spreckalmeyer (19881) *Evaluating Built Environments: A Behavioral Approach* (Ann Arbor, MI. : The University of Michigan, Institute for Social Research and College of Architecture and Urban Planning).

Newman, Oscar (1973) *Defensible Spaces: Crime Prevention through Urban Design* (New York: Collier Books).

Preiser, W. F. E. (1983) 'A Prototype Post-Occupancy Evaluation of the Agricultural Sciences Building-South at the University of Kentucky', in *Proceedings of the Conference on People and Physical Environment Research* (Wellington, NZ, 1983), edited by Duncan Joiner, Geoffrey Brimilcombe, John Daish, John Gray and David Kernohan, pp. 448–62 (Wellington: NZ Ministry of Works and Development).

Preiser, W. F. E., Rabinowitz, H. Z. and White, E. T. (1988) *Post Occupancy Evaluation* (New York: Van Nostrand Reinhold).

Rabinowitz, H. Z. (1975) *Buildings in Use Study* (Milwaukee, WI: University of Wisconsin, School of Architecture and Urban Planning).

Sanoff, H. (1978) *Designing with Community participation* (New York: McGraw-Hill).

Sanoff, H. (1979) *Design Games: playing for keeps with personal and environmental design decisions* (Los Altos, California: William Kaufmann).

Schneekloth, Lynda H (1987) 'Advances in practice in environment, behavior and design', in *Advances in Environment Behavior and Design*, edited by Ervin H. Zube and Gary T. Moore, Vol. 1, pp. 307–334 (New York: Plenum Books).

Schneekloth, L. and Shibley, R. (1981) 'On owning a piece of the rock', in *Design-Research Interactions: Exploring the Future through the 1980s: Proceedings of the Sixteenth Environmental Design Research Association Conference*, edited by Arvid E. Osterber, Carole Tiernan and Robert A. Findlay, p. ix (Ames, Iowa: EDRA).

Schneekloth, L. H. and Shibley, R. (1987) 'Research/Practice: Thoughts on an Interactive Paradigm', in *Proceedings of the American Association of Collegiate Schools of Architecture Annual Research Conference*, edited by R. Shibley (Washington, DC: AIA/ACSA Research Council).

Schneekloth, L. H., and Shibley, R. (1990) *Toward the Dialogic Practice of Building Evaluation* (Buffalo: The State University of New York at Buffalo School of Architecture and Planning and The Caucus Partnership).

Schon, Donald (1983) *The Reflective Practitioner: How Practitioners think in action* (New York: Basic Books).

Scott, Brent (1987) *Aesthetic Evaluation: a Comparison of Architects and Non-Architects* (Wellington: BArch Research Report, School of Architecture, Victoria University of Wellington).

Shibley, R. (1985) 'Building Evaluation in the Mainstream', *Environment and Behavior*, 17:1, pp. 7–24 (New York: Sage).

Shibley, R., and Schneekloth, L. H. (1988) 'Risking Collaboration: Professional Dilemmas in Evaluation and Design,' *The Journal of Architectural and Planning Research*, 5:4 (Winter).

Steele, F. I. (1973) *Physical Settings and Organizational Development* (Massachusetts: Addison-Wesley Publishers).

Vischer, Jacqueline (1989) *Environmental Quality in Offices* (New York: Van Nostrand Reinhold).

Vischer, Jacqueline and Cooper Marcus, Clare (1982) 'Design Awards: Who Cares?', in *Knowledge for Design: Proceedings of the Thirteenth Environmental Design Research Association Conference*, edited by P. Bart, A. Chen and G. Francescato, pp. 210–223 (Maryland: EDRA).

Wisner, Ben, Stea, David and Kruks, Sonia (1991) 'Participatory and Action Research Methods', in *Advances in Environment Behavior and Design*, edited by Ervin H. Zube and Gary T. Moore, Vol. 3, pp. 271–295 (New York: Plenum Books).

Zimring, Craig and Wener, Richard (1985) 'Evaluating Evaluation', *Environment and Behavior*, 17:1, Jan., pp. 97–117 (New York: Sage).

Zube, E. H., and Moore, G. T. (1987) 'Advances in Environment Behavior and Design', in *Advances in Environment, Behavior, and Design*, Vol. 1 edited by Ervin H. Zube and Gary T. Moore, Preface, pp. vii-xiii (New York: Plenum Press).

Index